Tales of Old Chesham

by

George Piggin

Highgate Publications (Beverley) Limited, 1993

British Library Cataloguing in Publication Data

Piggin, George
    Tales of Old Chesham
    I. Title
    942.597

    ISBN 0-948929-70-7

Copyright © George Piggin, 1993

Published by
Highgate Publications (Beverley) Ltd., 24 Wylies Road, Beverley, HU17 7AP
Telephone (0482) 866826

Printed by
Colourspec, Unit 7, Tokenspire Park, Hull Road, Woodmansey, Beverley, HU17 0TB
Telephone (0482) 864264

ISBN 0 948929 70 7

PREFACE

Some five years ago, a friend, the Leader of a Church Evening Meeting, being rather stuck for a Speaker, said to me 'you know a lot about Chesham, will you come along and tell us a few tales.' I duly obliged and from that time my name has been passed in an ever widening circle to Secretaries of various groups. I have now spoken on over one hundred occasions, and have bookings for the next year. I never realised that there were so many Meeting Groups in the Town and District!

On many occasions after speaking, I have been asked, "Have you written all this down?" and I finally decided that I would do something about it. The pages that follow are my effort.

I have been lucky in that I had much information passed down to me from my Mother and other members of my family; I have been Churchwarden of St Mary's for many years, and have acted as Custodian of the Parish Registers (which date back to 1538) for some twenty years. They contain a mine of information in addition to the bare facts of Baptism, Marriage and Burial, and I have gleaned much from them.

I know well that several books on Chesham have previously been published but I trust that this book contains facts which may be of interest to residents and others, together with pictures which have not, so far, appeared.

A few thanks: I am indebted to my daughter-in-law, Sarah, who has been my typist; to my good friend Ray East for many of the pictures and to my dear Wife for putting up with me for years when I have been expounding on various local topics.

George Piggin,
Amy Lane,
Chesham

MARKET SQUARE, CHESHAM

OLD CHESHAM

CHESHAM

Chesham has a long and interesting history as befits any town where traces of prehistoric and Roman occupation have been found.

We know that prehistoric man lived here as various implements have been found in and around many parts of the original settlement — around the Market Square principally and evidence of Flint Knapping has been found in the area.

The original site — deep in a valley — must be in what was the bed of an ancient river thousands of years ago as some parts of the town have a subsoil of clay and chalk which makes the laying of foundations for buildings rather difficult. Only recently, when preparing for the erection of the Town Clock, piles had to be driven down over 30 feet in order to find a firm base. Yet — not far away — a firm bed of gravel can be found just a foot or two under the surface.

Being tucked in its hollow — years ago referred to as 'Sleepy Hollow' — the town was, for centuries, very remote, and although only less than 30 miles from the centre of London, it might for centuries have been a million miles away.

But that has all now changed!

Early History and the Parish Church

The first written mention of Chesham was in 970 when Lady Elgiva in her will bequeathed land in the town but little real evidence began until the building of St Mary's Church. This is believed to have been started in about 1120 to 1140 and almost certainly replaced an early place of Christian worship — probably a wooden building — on the site. This in turn had replaced what appears to have been a Pagan meeting place as a large number of agglomerate or pudding stones are included in the foundations and in the walls. These probably formed a circle. The stones range in size from one weighing many tonnes under the east wall of the south porch down to those weighing only a few pounds which are included in the framework of the walls.

St Mary's was the Church of the Parish of Chesham Leicester, i.e. it was built by the Abbey of Leicester and the Priests were appointed from there.

There is also believed to have been a second Parish Church, that of Chesham Woburn, which was sited at the foot of Fullers Hill. Traces of an ancient building were unearthed when the present Thomas Harding School was built in 1910. This Church is believed to have been built about the same time as St Mary's but fell into disuse in the 14th Century. However, two vicars were appointed, one by each Abbey until 1660 and the two parishes were not united until 3rd July 1767. There are believed to have been early parsonage houses at both Mount Nugent (near Mount Nugent Farm) and also at the foot of Fullers Hill. The present rectory was built in about 1720. It was originally of three floors and a basement cellar but the top floor was removed in the major restoration of 1956. The present Church annexe in the grounds of the rectory was originally two cottages for the domestic staff and was joined to the rectory by an overhead bridge. The Rectory itself is built within the area of the ancient Churchyard which extended down to the pair of iron gates near the foot of the cobbled driveway.

All the area of this driveway, and the various public and private footpaths through the

PUDDING (OR AGGLOMERATE) STONE UNDER SOUTH PORCH OF ST. MARY'S

Churchyard are the sites of ancient graves — probably used some 400-500 years ago.

The original St Mary's was a cruciform building. The outside walls were situated where the two rows of pillars now stand. The Chancel was much shorter than at present and the roof considerably lower. The only trace remaining of this early building is part of the tracery of a small lancet window in the wall at the front of the north aisle. This originally let the daylight into the north transept. As the Parish grew so the Church was extended. The north aisle was added in the middle of the 13th Century and the south aisle and porch some 100 years later. Galleries were erected at the turn of the 16/1700's along the north and south sides, one for men and one for women. A minstrels gallery was erected over the west door. These were all removed in the 1868/9 restoration although the Minstrels gallery had by that time long since been disused, the minstrels having been dismissed for drunken and unruly behaviour in the early 1700's when the first organ was installed.

STRUT FROM GALLERY IN ST MARY'S CHURCH (ERECTED 1700, DEMOLISHED 1868)

Old Properties in the Town

Apart from St Mary's Church, the oldest remaining property is 54 Church Street, which was originally built as a Fourteenth Century Hall House. This was of one room only, in which the whole family lived, ate and slept. The floor was of trodden earth, with a fire in the middle, above which, on an iron frame, hung the inevitable Cooking Pot. Smoke from the fire made its way up and out through the thatched roof, there being no such thing as a chimney. Is it any wonder that the mortality rate was high? At this time, if you survived infancy (which a high proportion did not) the expectation of life was about 35 years. Later, such houses had upper storeys inserted, fireplaces built and a proper floor laid. No. 54 has, of course, been modernised inside, but the facia retains its original appearance.

There are many other houses in Church Street of the Fifteenth and Sixteenth Centuries, now jealously preserved as part of the Conservation Area. The small triangle containing houses Nos 37 to 47 was originally the site of the Bide Well, or Holy Well where parishioners coming from far flung parts of the Parish (it is some 25 square miles) to worship at St Mary's would wash and refresh themselves before entering the Church.

Church Street was, for many years, the centre of commerce of the town. A century ago it contained 8 pubs plus How's Brewery (now Nos 80-82) which had a beer shop on the street side.

The town's first proper Post Office was set up at No 28 in the early 19th Century. Prior to this date, letters were handed in at the George Public House in the High Street, where the landlord was also Postmaster. You paid the necessary fee —

OLD PROPERTIES IN CHURCH STREET, 1890-1900

depending on how far the letter was to go — and by means of various carriers by coach and horseback it eventually arrived at its destination.

Only 75 years ago there were 3 Butchers, 2 Bakers, 2 Grocers, a Tailor and a Bootmaker in the Street, the High Street at the time contained many private houses — all the "Best people" lived there!!

The premises on the corner of Pednor Road — lately an Antique Shop — was originally the Toll House, where tolls were paid on the road to Great Missenden; it was later the One Bell Public House . . . later still an Off Licence.

Early Population Estimates

The first reliable estimate of the population dwelling within the parish — one of the largest in England — can be deduced from the first parish register which was brought into use in 1538. At that time the population is believed to have been around 1,000 of whom half lived in the town — principally the two streets which are now High Street and Church Street and the other half lived in the seven hamlets. These were Bellingdon, Asheridge, Chartridge, Hundridge, Botley, Ashley Green and Waterside. There were three chapels of ease — at Hundridge this was dedicated to St Edmund the Martyr and still stands in the grounds of Great Hundridge Manor although long since deconsecrated). There was a second chapel at Grove in Grove Lane and a third possibly at Botley although no traces of this last remain. The parish was a poor agricultural area almost completely self-contained. All food required was of course grown on the farms and in gardens. Wool from the sheep was spun and woven into cloth for the manufacture of clothing and leather from the hide of cattle was tanned and made into footwear. A travelling packman would have visited the town probably twice a year on horseback with his wares, possibly rudimentary jewellery, needles, pins, buttons etcetera. He would have stayed two or three nights in one of the many local hostelries and then passed on his way to his next call, either Amersham in one direction or Hemel Hempstead in the other.

Rivalry with Amersham

In the Twentieth Century rivalry with our neighbours in Amersham is probably confined to the sporting field. This was by no means always so. In the early years of the Christian Church all parishioners were expected to go in pilgrimage to their Cathedral on the Monday following Whit Sunday in each year. Chesham at the time was in the diocese of Lincoln, rather too far for a day's walk so the Bishop of Lincoln permitted the parishioners to go in procession to the parish Church at Amersham. There, with other visitors, they circled the Church in procession before entering for the necessary service. Fierce arguments broke out between the parties from Chesham and Amersham as to who should take precedence in the procession and who should carry the banners. For some years in the early 1400s the annual event was marred by fights. Many casualties are said to have ensued. In 1454 the parishioners of Chesham could stand this no longer and petitioned the Bishop to be allowed to make their pilgrimage at their own Church. This the Bishop granted providing that the Parish pay 1s and 4d (7p in today's currency) to the upkeep of Lincoln Cathedral. So far as is known this condition is still in existence although no payment has been made in living memory.

The following entries from the Parish Registers may also add weight:-

"Confirmed by the Bishop of Lincoln at the Parish Church of Amersham on Monday the 10th day of May in the Year 1773, 104 young people of this Parish with Certificates from me." (Signed) W. Hoggart, Curate.

Also

"Confirmed by the Right Reverend the Lord Bishop of Lincoln at Amersham on Monday the 24th day of 8 June 1791, 204 young persons of this Parish with Certificates from me." (Signed) F. Bowen, Curate.

Why did such large numbers of Candidates have to walk to Amersham? We did not owe allegiance to Amersham at the time. We must remember that, being in Lincoln Diocese, well over 100 miles away, the Bishop only visited us every three or four years. His visits created quite a stir in the Town with the Church bells being rung to herald his arrival.

He of course arrived by horse and carriage, and spent at least one night at the Rectory before proceeding on his Tour.

Fierce rivalry was still in existence until less than a century ago when, on the occasion of Amersham Fair (19th September), the Chesham lads went en masse with the sole object of picking a fight, which they usually won, for, as they descended Rectory Hill into Amersham they gathered various missiles from the banks alongside the road, with which to pelt the unfortunate locals who were on a lower level.

Only a century ago it was always said that Chesham and Amersham men and women should not intermarry — there was sure to be trouble if they did! I think that this has now died out but there is still a certain amount of jealousy in Chesham over the fact that the Council Offices, Police Station, Magistrates Court, Social Services Department and several other Public offices are all in Amersham!

Thomas Harding the Local Martyr

During the Tudor period many protestants (let us remember that England was still a Roman Catholic country) suffered death and persecution for their beliefs. As early as 1506, in the reign of King Henry VII, Thomas Harding was persecuted for speaking against the idolatry and superstition of the Roman Catholic Church. He was sentenced to make penance, and to wear a faggot on his sleeve, branding him as a heretic. He was banished to live in Amersham with his wife Alice. In 1515 the penance was terminated but he was ordered not to live outside the parish of Amersham and to go on an annual pilgrimage for his sins on Corpus Christi day to the Religious house (the college of Bon Hommes at Asheridge near Berkhamstead). In 1522 he was permitted to return to Chesham. He lived in a house on the site of which the present number 60 Broadway is built although his house stood back from the road fronted by the infant river Chess which to this day passes underground at this site. He farmed lands at Dungrove on the strip farming system which was the current vogue at the time. Nothing further was heard of him until 1532 when he was apprehended whilst sitting on a stile alternatively described as at the entrance to Hodds Wood or at the entrance to Beech Wood where he was reading religious books in English which was considered heresy at the time. He was tried before the court of Bishop Longland of Lincoln and sentenced to death by burning. He was kept in the parvise (room over the south porch of St Mary's Church) on the night of 28th May 1532 whilst the Vicar preached a Sermon against him. The next night he spent in prayer at his home in the Broadway. This house was only demolished in 1870. On 30th May he was taken in procession to a dell at the foot of White Hill (at the entrance to the present White Hill Centre) where a fire had been

THOMAS HARDING MEMORIAL

prepared and a large post erected. To this he was affixed and the fire kindled. Before the flames could engulf him a bystander threw a block of wood which hit Harding on the side of the head and killed him. A cry went up from the large assembled crowd stating, "There goes a true Christian man." A memorial cross was erected to Thomas Harding's memory in St Mary's Churchyard in 1908. It is inscribed:-

> "To the Glory of God and to the
> memory of Thomas Harding of
> Dungrove Chesham who in fiery trial
> at the stake laid down his life for
> the word of God and for the testimony
> of Jesus Christ in this Parish on
> May 30th 1532"

There is an inscription underneath this which reads:-

> "The noble army of martyrs praise thee"

He was no doubt buried in the Churchyard but as this was some six years before the commencement of Parish Registers the site of his grave cannot be ascertained.

Restoration of St Mary's

Little had been done in the way of restoration and repair of the parish Church from the time of its completion in its present form in 1445 until the early 1600's. In 1606 the vicar, Richard Bowle, decided that his Church was in a "broken and parlous state", stonework was dilapidated and such seating as there was was old and broken and not fit for decent folk to sit upon, so he decided to set about the restoration of the building. At this period every parishioner was officially a member of the parish Church and the Church authorities were entitled to make a levy on the population for its upkeep. This Richard Bowle decided to do. There were 347 families residing in the parish at the time. Of these 170 made a contribution and 177 failed to respond. Those responding contributed the then considerable sum of £114 16s 5d. With this amount Richard Bowle set

about the work. Everything was carefully written down by him in a book which survives in the Church to this day. The money unfortunately ran out before work was completed and a further levy was made on the families who had already contributed. This raised the sum of £30 which enabled the work to be finished, proper box pews to be installed and the stone work put into good order. The 177 families who did not contribute obviously "got away with it" as no further mention of them is made.

From the number of families in the Parish at the time — 347 — it is deduced allowing for about 7 per family — that the population had risen to around 2000 by this time — a considerable rise from the 1000 estimated some 68 years earlier in 1538.

From 1606 on the population grew but slowly and 200 years later — the early 1800's — had reached about 6000. When industrialisation came — just over 100 years ago — it put on a "spurt" to some 8500 as folk moved in to work in the new factories. There it remained until after the 1939/45 War when, with the big building boom whereby houses were built for folk moving in, principally from the London and Middlesex area — the figure rose in some 20 years to over 20,000.

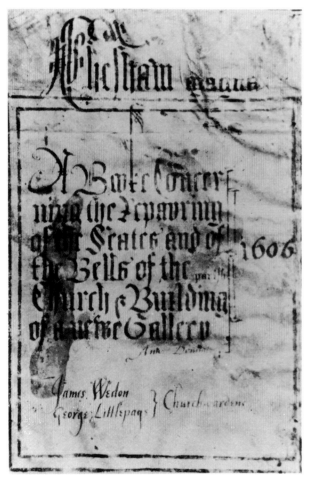

RICHARD BOWLE'S BOOK

Puritans who left Chesham for the New World

Chesham had two families who were members of the Puritans who wished to free themselves from the religious quarrels which followed the Reformation. The first of the Puritans sailed in the Mayflower to America in 1620 and within the next ten years some 2,000 had left. The two Chesham families who were among the first brave souls who faced the terrors of the Atlantic for the sake of their conscience and faith were the Sale family and the Chase family. The Sale family settled in Connecticut and the family remain in that area to this day being able to trace a direct link to their ancestors in Chesham. The Chase family spread to most parts of the United States and were the originators of the Chase Manhattan Bank which now has branches in most of the Capital cities of the world. The family lived at Hundridge Farm, now Great Hundridge Manor and to this day members of the family still visit Chesham every summer. They are keen to inspect the Baptismal Register containing the record of the Baptism of Aquila Chase (a male!) in 1582, who was the emigrant who started it all! Needless to say numerous offers have been made to purchase this Register which, of course, have all been turned down — but photographs of the page concerned have been regularly taken. They are very keen to retain their links with the town. Many of the family made good in the United States — there is a story of a marriage with the Rockefellers and two books have been written and published in the States detailing the many members of the family. At the time of their occupation of Hundridge Farm it was a small working farmstead. The Chapel of St Edmund the Martyr which was built alongside

CHAPEL OF ST EDMUND THE MARTYR, HUNDRIDGE

Hundridge for the members of that small community to take part in public worship still stands to this day in its original form although long since deconsecrated.

Rise of Non Conformity in the District

Chesham was well to the fore in the rise of Non-conformity in this country and indeed has right until the present day been a considerable stronghold. As early as 1676 a joint Baptist church for Chesham and Berkhamstead was formed, its whereabouts are unknown. In 1706 Chesham members formed a church of their own meeting in one of the homes but building their own meeting house in 1712 on the site of the present Broadway Baptist Church which was erected in 1902. Hinton Baptist Church, the present building built only in 1898, originally dated back to 1701 when a few members calling themselves Particular Baptists worshipped in a private house. The first meeting house which they built commenced in 1719. The Independent Chapel which later became the Congregational Church in the Broadway was erected in 1724 and was replaced by the present building in 1886. The strict Baptists worshipped in a church in Townfield Yard which was built in 1820 and from that date until 1934 Chesham boasted the unique siting of three Baptist churches on one acre of land in Red Lion Street and Townfield Yard. The strict Baptist church became disused in 1934 on the building of the Berkhamstead Road Baptist Church now known as Newtown Evangelical Church. Members of the Hinton Church suffered a difference of opinion in 1868 and a breakaway faction erected Zion Church a few yards away. The original Methodist Church known as the Wesleyan Chapel was built in Broad Street in 1897 and a few yards away the Salvation Army Barracks was erected a year later. Following a dispute among members of the Broadway Baptist Church a breakaway faction formed the United Free Church in Bellingdon Road which stood on the site of the present Methodist church. The minister was the well-known Rev. Walter Wynn, widely renowned as a firebrand preacher and a great character in the town and district. The Quaker Meeting House in Bellingdon Road was in existence as early as 1678 when the road was known as Quaker Lane. Rumour has it that Oliver Cromwell attended Divine Service there. During the great plague of 1665 Richard Baxter, a well known Quaker preached at the Quaker Meeting House in Amersham, records showing that he maintained controversy for a whole day "with certain giddy minds from Chesham". Several troopers of the local militia were present during the day but whether they were there to keep the peace between the belligerent parties or to take part in the lengthy discussion is not recorded. The Plymouth Brethren meeting house in Station Road, now known as the Gospel Hall was erected in 1890. There was, in the 1920's and 1930's a small Methodist meeting house next to the White Lion Pub in Townfield Yard but this was never a proper church in its own right. The Non-conformists of the town were certainly an outward looking band in spite of their differences as outlined above. A Baptist Chapel was built at Chesham Vale, two at Ashley Green, one at Whelpley Hill, two at Hyde Heath, one at Chartridge and a Congregational Chapel at Asheridge. Only Chartridge and Hyde Heath now have chapels of which the latter, known as the Union Chapel, was the result of the coming together of the two small Baptist chapels in the village.

Churchyard and Burial Grounds

St Mary's Churchyard — and the interior of the Church — were used as the Parish Burial Ground

OLD INDEPENDENT CHAPEL

OLD BROADWAY BAPTIST CHAPEL

OLD HINTON CHAPEL

OLD TOWNFIELD CHAPEL

from the very earliest days up until 1858. Although as indicated elsewhere, no record was made of these until 1538, it is estimated that some 70,000 burials took place there over a period of some thousand years, and the likelihood is that the area was used up to three times during this period. Until comparatively recently in history, few persons were buried in coffins, and the Verger would use his verge (or staff) to prod the ground to find a vacant space.

There are a number of entries in the Parish Records mentioning persons being buried within the Church — let us remember that for centuries the floor was only of trodden earth — and it seems that this practice was almost exclusively reserved for the Gentry of the Parish — the more money you left the nearer to the Altar you were buried. In 1858, the Vicar and Churchwardens decided that enough was enough and on 21st December of that year the Bishop came to Chesham declaring the Churchyard full and dedicating the new Cemetery in Bellingdon Road and after that only persons whose family had a vault or brick grave with space remaining could be buried in the Churchyard, the last interment being in 1934. Several of the Non-Conformist Chapels had their own small Burial Grounds, and of these two remain in existence, one in Bellingdon Road and the other in Punchbowl Lane, together with the Quaker Burial Ground in Bellingdon Road and a few graves behind Broadway Baptist and United Reformed Churches.

Early Schools in the Town

During the 18th Century several rudimentary schools were established by private individuals in their homes. Most of these were the traditional straw plaiting schools where children as young as 4 or 5 years of age were taught to split and plait straw which was then collected by a travelling representative from one of the many hat factories in Luton. The children paid a few coppers each week for their tuition which usually comprised reading of the Bible and simple arithmetic. The children could earn a few coppers from their plaiting, the usual fee was three pence for 12 yards. In the early 19th Century private schools were established for the tuition of the 3 "R's". One was in the building which until recently contained Chesham Post Office, one in the building formerly on the site of the present Post Office and one last one in Waterside. The first free school in the town was erected in 1828 by public subscription in Townfield Yard for the tuition of 150 boys. The building still stands in its original form — and it is now a printing works — and one wonders how 150 boys could possibly have even got into the building let alone received any

OLD NATIONAL SCHOOL (1828)

tuition. The Church of England school in Church Street was erected in 1845. To accommodate this a block of five cottages known as the Church Houses had to be demolished. The school was for both

OLD CHURCH SCHOOL (1845)

sexes, boys one side of the screen, girls the other, and the children were all taught together from the age of 5 or 6 when they enrolled until the age of 11 or 12 when either they or their parents felt that they had received sufficient education and that it was about time they left to earn some money. There was no official school leaving age at this time. The girls' half of the building contained one iron heating stove in the corner but the boys' half contained no heating at all. A school entitling itself Chesham Grammar School opened at 37 Germain Street in the 1850's. This building was half of Chesham's former workhouse and accommodated both boarding and day boys. The school was only in existence for a fairly short space of time. The first public elementary school in the town was Waterside Girls' School built in 1864 in memory of the late Lord Chesham which stood on a site just below the present Chessmount Rise. Townsend Road School was commenced in 1878 and enlarged to its fuller size some twenty years later. Whitehill School (now the Community Centre) and Thomas Harding School were both built in the early 1900's and the rest of today's schools were all erected in the period following the 1939-45 War.

Chesham and its Mineral Spring

In 1820 a Chalybeate or Iron-bearing spring was discovered in Amersham Road (by the site of the present petrol filling station). A group of local businessmen decided to exploit this spring as other such springs were at the time being exploited in Leamington, Droitwich, Matlock, Tunbridge Wells and sundry other spa towns throughout the country. A building was erected alongside the spring (now known as Mineral Cottage) in 1821 where the water was to be dispensed and Mineral House in Mineral

MINERAL COTTAGE

Lane was erected to provide accommodation for those coming from afar to take the waters. Unfortunately, a few years later the spring ran dry. This was the end of a venture which might well have put our town on a par with many of the major spa towns of England. The spring re-appeared in later years but the taking of the waters had somewhat gone out of fashion and the outflow was channelled into watercress beds on the same site which were only filled in within living memory.

Chesham and its Railway

Chesham was very late in receiving its railway. Berkhamstead was connected to London and the Midlands as early as 1835 and from that date onwards a horse-drawn carriage left the George Hotel in the High Street to travel to Berkhamstead to meet most of the trains passing through, about 4 a day in each direction. Rickmansworth received its station on the old LMS railway some 10 years later

HORSE BUS TO BERKHAMSTED

AN EARLY TRAIN AT CHESHAM

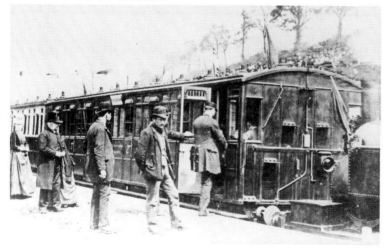

*BANQUET TO CELEBRATE THE ARRIVAL
OF THE RAILWAY*

and a carrier then operated to that town. The railway finally reached Chesham in 1889, the spur from Rickmansworth through Chorleywood and Chalfont Road being pushed on to Chesham in that year. The original site for the station was selected on Chesham Moor (the site of the present Moor allotments) and to this day this land is still owned by British Rail. There was a move by local people to have the station brought nearer to the centre of the town which resulted in it being built on its present site. The original intention was that the line should continue via Victoria Road, Brockhurst Road and the Vale to Hawridge, Tring and so on through Aylesbury to the Midlands. Land was purchased for the project but when the Rail Authorities tried to buy land in the vicinity of Tring, Lord Rothschild who owned virtually all that town and its surroundings refused to sell any land so the Metropolitan and Great Central Railway decided that they would approach Aylesbury from Chalfont Road through Amersham, Great Missenden and Wendover. However, does hope still spring eternal? In 1992 British Rail still owns a large tract of land in Chesham Vale. The coming of the railway in May 1889 was celebrated by a mammoth banquet to which a thousand townsfolk and visiting dignitaries were invited. The meal was of the gargantuan size of the time and lasted some four hours. The official opening of the railway to the public was in July 1889 when four trains in each direction connected Chesham to London, the journey time being just over the hour.

The Bury

The Bury in Church Street — next to St Mary's Church — is and has been for many years, the largest house in the Town, although regretfully no longer in private occupation.

The original house on the site was built in the early 1700s (it has since been enlarged) and was, for over two hundred years the home of the Lowndes family. An early member of the family held the office of Chancellor of the Exchequer under the King, at the time of course when the King played a much more active part in the running of the Country than is the case with the Monarchy today, and for his services was granted a Coat of Arms with the motto "Ways and Means", as he is said to have found ways and means of getting the King out of financial trouble.

Early members of the family are commemorated in Stained Glass Windows in the Chancel of St Mary's, and several of the Hatchments on the walls of the South Transept and South Aisle are to the family. They include one to William Lowndes who died in 1905, such Hatchment being one of only a very few Twentieth Century Hatchments in the Country — they had rather gone out of fashion by this time.

As stated elsewhere in this book, the family were deposed from The Bury at the outbreak of War in 1939, and never returned to live there. A large hutted camp was built in the grounds, and at the cessation of hostilities in 1945 the house and grounds were in rather a sad and sorry state. The house and buildings next became a turkey breeding establishment, which flourished for some years, then closed down. In the 1950s The Bury, together with fourteen acres of land, was offered to Chesham Urban District Council for the sum of £27,500. It was suggested that it would make admirable Council offices and amenity land, but in what must have been one of the worst decisions ever made by Chesham Council, they turned the offer down! The whole lot was then bought by Tyne and Wear County Council (300 miles away) as an investment for their Pension Fund. Today, the building and grounds are beautifully restored and maintained,

The Bury, Chesham.

THE BURY

and are occupied by a firm of Solicitors and other businesses. What an opportunity was missed! Chesham was called 'Sleepy Hollow' at one time; I wonder why?

The Curfew Bell

Chesham was one of the last towns in the country in which the curfew bell was rung from the tower of the Parish Church. This was in operation every week night from Michaelmas through to Easter. The bell was tolled for 15 minutes at 8pm in order that the good folk of the town should know that it was time to put out their fires, extinguish their lights and retire to bed. The origin of the custom in the Middle Ages when most houses comprised a large element of timber and thatch was obviously a very good one but by 1939 it had become something of a curiosity. The verger of the Church ascended the tower each night and carefully tolled one of the bells for 15 minutes followed, after an interval, by striking the number of strokes that there were days in the month in order that the townsfolk should know the date. I accompanied him on his task as a small boy many times in the 1920's. When the date was early in the month the tolling of the date bell posed few problems but when it was the end of the month and 29, 30 or 31 strokes had to be tolled, the verger always asked for complete silence in the ringing chamber in order that he could accurately count the number of strokes. The curfew was rung for the last time at Easter 1939, by Michaelmas of that year war had been declared and all church bells were silenced for the duration. With the ending of the war in 1945 the custom was never reinstated. I rather think it would be difficult to obtain the services of a ringer at 8pm six nights every week in these days.

The Fire Service in Chesham

Prior to 1840 there was no organised fire brigade as we know it today in the town. Certain insurance companies, mainly Sun Life, maintained some rudimentary system of men who would attend a fire at your house if you were insured by the appropriate company and a few houses in the town to this day still bear fire marks on their front walls. It was said that if your house caught fire and you were not insured with the Company concerned they would still attend on payment of a fee of £5. At the time of course this was a considerable sum of money and the story goes that many a house holder finding his or her house on fire would run round to relatives, friends and neighbours borrowing half a crown here and a shilling there to try and raise the necessary sum. Story has it that in most cases by the time the sum had been raised the house had been burnt out

anyway. The first fire brigade under the auspices of the local government board — the forerunner of local councils — was organised in 1840. The fire "engine" — a hand pump — was housed in a shed in Wey Lane. It was pulled to the site of the fire by horses belonging to How's brewery of Church Street which were kept in a field near by the engine house. These horses were so knowledgeable that when they heard the bell in the town hall being tolled for a fire they ran to the gate of the field and waited to be harnessed to the fire engine. This early engine was superseded several times by improved models. The last horse-drawn engine, a fine machine with a massive brass boiler was housed in a building in High Street and was used until 1923. The first fireman to arrive at the station following the tolling of the bell had the duty to light the fire underneath the boiler in order that a head of steam could be raised to operate the pump. If the fire was some distance from the station all was well as there was time for the water to boil and steam to be raised but I can remember well seeing this fire engine drawn out for the last time to a fire at the High Street end of Church Street, less than two minutes run from the fire station. When the engine arrived at the site of the fire they had to stand in idleness for some time until steam was raised and the pump could be operated. The first motor engine was purchased for the town in 1923. It was a magnificent solid tyred Leyland Vehicle named Norah after the wife of Ralph Howard, Chief Officer of the brigade. So proud were the firemen of their new engine that it was decided that it should be shown off to the people of the town. The High Street was therefore closed on a Saturday evening whilst the engine took up its position at the foot of Station Road and proceeded to squirt water to the four corners of the Broadway. The farthest jets reached almost up to the former Post Office (between the United Reformed Church and Lloyds Bank). Hundreds of townsfolk turned out for this spectacle

HORSE DRAWN FIRE ENGINE AT THE BURY (1900)

FIRST MOTOR FIRE ENGINE (1923)

and warmly applauded the efforts of the firemen. At the conclusion of the demonstration the Broadway was awash, fortunately at this time there was very little traffic. In 1931 the fire brigade at Great Missenden for some reason or other went on strike and refused to attend any fires. It was decided that Chesham with its up to date engine would cover any fires breaking out in the Missenden area and shortly after the strike began one evening a call came through from Great Missenden. It was a winter evening and in the darkness the fire engine raced along Missenden Road which at the time was no more than a narrow winding country lane. When it reached the sharp turn by Lower Hundridge the driver failed to negotiate the bend in the road and the engine careered straight ahead through the hedge and into a field, overturning and throwing off all the men. Fortunately nothing more than a few cuts and bruises resulted but the engine was unable to proceed to the fire. In war time the fire service was re-enforced with auxiliary vehicles which were equipped to deal with incendiary bombs and for rescue of persons from property damaged by bombing. After the end of the war Chesham had two very fine motor fire engines which were in existence until very recently when, as most people know, we were demoted to one engine and a small tender.

Chesham and the Four B's

Chesham was long known as the town of the four B's — Beer, Boots, Brushes and Baptists.

BEER

Beer was, for many years, indeed until the 1950's brewed at Chesham Brewery, which sat at the foot of White Hill, and earlier also at How's Brewery in Church Street. In the late 1800's there was considerable rivalry between the two although Chesham Brewery, locally known as Nash's, was by far the larger and supplied considerably more public houses. How's brewery closed down in the early years of this century when its public houses were taken over by Chesham Brewery. This in turn in the 1930's amalgamated with Brackley Brewery and was known as the Chesham and Brackley Brewery Company. The company was later taken over by Ind Coope, later again becoming Ind Coope Tetley Ansell and currently Allied Breweries. The Brewery buildings which stood on both sides at the foot of White Hill were demolished in the 1960's. The road was widened and the building formerly occupied by A.C.T. was erected on the larger part of the site, Gladstone Court being erected on the smaller part. A deep well on the premises of Chesham Brewery supplied the necessary pure spring water which was always said to give the locally brewed brands their distinctive flavour. How's brewery, although situated in Church Street, where No 82 is now on the site, had an off-licence attached and its malt house was in Tap Yard off the High Street. This was my great grandfather's property and my grandmother often told the story of how, as a young girl she served customers with their supper beer. The custom was to bring a quart jug for a supper pint — price one penny — and the jug had to be filled with both a pint measure and a half pint measure in order that the customers received value for money. Beer was supplied by both breweries to their many public houses in the town and surrounding district in the traditional 4 ½ gallon, 9 gallon, 18 gallon and 36 gallon wooden barrels. Beer, of course, was not packed under pressure at the time and if the barrels were opened and the weather was warm there was always the problem of keeping the beer in good condition and in summer time the barrels were always wrapped in a damp white cloth.

CHESHAM BREWERY (DEMOLISHED 1952)

BOOTS

Boot making, of the heavy variety, was, from the time of the industrial revolution, always a busy industry in Chesham. At the turn of the century there were some 8 manufacturers in the town, some in large factories employing 50 or more hands, others in small work-shops tucked away in yards employing only half a dozen. The complete boot was made in these factories, i.e. the upper, inner and outer soles were all cut from sheet leather on the premises. There originally existed a tanning mill in Water Lane — which was originally a corn mill and

BOOT FACTORY, HIGHAM ROAD

which was later to become a woodenwear factory and this mill obtained the hides from local slaughter houses, put them through the tanning process and supplied the finished leather to the local factories. So the whole boot could really be said to be Chesham made. Now, in 1993, only Messrs Gifford Newton of Townsend Road keep the flag flying. The demise was partly because of the failure of the factories to go over to shoe manufacture when it became the fashion for working people to wear shoes as distinct from the heavy type of sturdy boots which were always worn by the working men in the Victorian era.

BRUSHES

In its heyday the brush trade in Chesham was carried on in upwards of a dozen factories and every conceivable type of brush from a small paint brush up to a large wooden broom was made, most of

BRUSH FACTORY, HIGHAM ROAD

which were despatched to the far corners of the country and indeed to parts of Europe. The beech stocks were cut from locally felled timber but the bristle always had to be imported, usually from the Orient. With the introduction of nylon several factories went over to this type of manufacture but gradually because of fierce competition from others one after the other closed down until today, we find the flag only being flown by Messrs Russells of Townsend Road who still manufacture the traditional type of bristle brush.

BAPTISTS

The town has long since been a stronghold of the Baptist way of worship and the earliest Baptist meeting house was set up before 1700. By 1900 there were 4 Baptist Churches in the town, later increasing to a fifth when the Chesham Free Church in Bellingdon Road was established as a breakaway from Broadway Baptist. Even today in 1993 we still have four Baptist Churches in the town, the same number as we have Anglican Churches. At the turn of the century it was estimated that half the population belonged to one or other of the Baptist Chapels, the remainder being members of the Anglican Church and other Non-conformist sects.

The Town Windmill

Like most towns and villages in the Chilterns, Chesham possessed a fine smock mill which was situated in the grounds of the Mansion known as Bury Hill which of course stood in what is now Chesham Park. The windmill was situated on a piece of land known locally as the Rolling Pin at the top of the ridge above the bowling green. For many years the windmill worked in conjunction with the five water mills on the River Chess but in the early 1800's it became disused and decay set in. In 1821 it was sold to the village of Lacey Green near Princes Risborough and was demolished and carried on carts piece by piece to that village where

CHESHAM WINDMILL (BUILT 1650)

it was re-erected, put into working order and destined to grind corn until 1950. It then once more fell into disuse, indeed 20 years later it was little more than a ruin. In the 1970's the Chiltern Preservation Society took over the Mill, and set about restoration. After several years' work mainly by volunteers the mill was once again restored to working order and now on summer weekends in the year is open to the public and is a fine asset to the countryside around Lacey Green. What a pity that it was sold from Chesham, as what a fine sight it would be on the skyline of the park today.

Law and Order

For many years up until the coming of a proper police force in the mid 1800's responsibility for law and order in the town rested with the parish constable who was appointed by the annual Vestry

POLICE STATION, BROAD STREET

Meeting. The stocks, pillory and cage for the incarceration of felons were all situated in the centre of what is now known as Chesham Broadway and until these were demolished in 1833 the area was known as "Pillory Green". The first police station as we know it today was situated in Amy Lane and there was a small lock-up attached. Anyone sentenced to more than 7 days in jail was sent in the care of the local constable to the County Jail at Aylesbury and the story exists that on one occasion as a prisoner was being conveyed to the County Jail in horse and trap a wheel came off the vehicle in Great Missenden near the Black Horse pub. The constable, after some thought decided that he would have to return on horseback to Chesham to obtain another cart but he entrusted his prisoner to the care of the Landlord of the public house obtaining from the prisoner a promise that he would not abscond but that he could drink as much beer as he wished during the constable's absence. On return from Chesham with a new cart some hours later the constable was horrified to find that the prisoner had consumed no fewer than 32 pints of beer for which the constable had to pay. The next police station was built in the 1890's in Broad Street, opposite Townsend Road. This was superseded by a much larger building with courthouse attached in the early 1930's. In turn this building has recently become disused as the bulk of Chesham's police work is now centred on Amersham but the town does still boast a small Police Station built in the 1980's alongside the previous station in Broad Street, which has now been converted into offices.

Chesham and its Workhouses

The original Chesham workhouse to cater for the poor and infirm of the town was erected in the mid 1500s in Germain Street. The building still exists, being Nos. 74 and 76 and now comprises two separate houses. The original building housed only some 20 or so inmates and even they must have been somewhat crowded and the able bodied among them were put to work in the workhouse gardens, a small portion of which is still in existence today on the corner of Germain Street and Wey Lane. By the early 1700's the number of paupers in the parish had outgrown the existing workhouse and a fine new building was erected at Nos 35, 37 Germain Street., the workhouse Master's house being next door at No 33. This fine three storey building housed the paupers of the parish until the poor law act of 1837 which grouped together fourteen parishes as the "Amersham Union". A fine new building — now the older part of Amersham General Hospital — known as the Union Workhouse was erected in what was a central position of the district. The move of the paupers from Chesham to Amersham was resented by both paupers and their relatives who felt that their loved ones were being sent far far away. On the day appointed for the move — the able-bodied were of course expected to walk to Amersham — the paupers were turned out of the Germain Street building and staged a protest known as the Chesham Riot on the southern side of the bridge over the River Chess. They flatly refused to walk the necessary three miles. Captain Fuller who lived at Germains in Fullers Hill was an officer of the Bucks Militia, an early type of TA/Home Guard. Captain Fuller tried to reason with the paupers but they would have none of it. He therefore despatched a rider to Aylesbury where a troop of militia were quartered and they arrived in the town some two days later. After considerable pressure and vociferous protest the paupers realised that their cause was a lost one and they proceeded to Amersham after further argument. The fine building in Germain Street was split into two parts

*ORIGINAL PARISH
WORKHOUSE*

*SECOND PARISH
WORKHOUSE*

and number 37 became Chesham Grammar School for boys — a private establishment. Both boarders and day boys were catered for and public examinations were undertaken. The school only survived some 20 years and since that date the former workhouse has been two rather gracious private houses.

Typhoid Epidemic

In 1871 a virulent outbreak of Typhoid, always referred to locally as the Chesham plague, broke out in Hearne's Yard, now known as Bury Lane, off Church Street. The outbreak was in a row of cottages long since demolished which obtained their water supply from the traditional well in the back yard. This well was immediately adjacent to the Rectory garden which was originally part of the Church Yard and water from the Church Yard obviously seeped down the slope into this well carrying with it the residue from various illnesses which had caused the deaths of those buried there and the well was obviously heavily contaminated. The outbreak spread rapidly down Church Street and into the High Street and affected people living in various yards and alleys off these two streets. At the time there was only one Doctor in the town and this was, of course, before the days of District Nurses. Two nurses were brought from one of the London Hospitals to tend the sick but in a short space of time both contracted the disease and died. Within the space of some three weeks 29 people died from the disease which caused tremendous fear and apprehension among people living in the part of the town concerned. The Rector, the Reverend Adolphus Aylward did his utmost in visiting the sick and taking them food and money. He too contracted the disease and was indeed the last to die from it. The disease abated as quickly as

it had arrived and many people who had been seriously ill in due course recovered. The bodies of those who died in the outbreak were all interred in Chesham cemetery which had been opened some

MEMORIAL TO REV. ADOLPHUS AYLWARD

13 years earlier and are not buried in the triangular piece of St Mary's Churchyard opposite the Rectory which local hearsay would have it. The St Mary's Churchyard had been closed for burials in 1858 and after that date only persons having space in a family vault or brick grave could claim right of burial there.

Yards and Alleys

Like most English towns Chesham contained a considerable number of Yards and Alleys, principally running off High Street and Church Street. Off High Street ran White Lion Yard, Townfield Yard, Stratfords Yard, Chequers Yard, Lewins Yard, Francis Yard, Lum's Yard, Tap Yard, Star Yard, Collins Alley, Huntsman Yard and Wagon Yard. Off Church Street ran Parsonage Lane,

TOWNFIELD YARD

DUCK ALLEY

Hearne's Yard (later Bury Lane), Mitchells Yard, Adams Alley and Reynold's Yard. Off Germain Street ran Duck Square, Duck Alley and Duck Yard. Off Blucher Street ran Star Yard. Of all these yards only Reynold's now contains dwellings. Most of the others were systematically demolished under the slum clearance act in the 1930's and the inhabitants moved to the newly built Pond Park

Estate. Most of them did not take kindly to their new surroundings at the top of a very steep hill having been used previously to being on top of shops, pubs and all other services in the centre of the town. Today, when one visits many English country towns one sees Yards and Alleys which have been transformed into delightful mews cottages with a few tubs of flowers and window boxes one feels that this could almost certainly have been the case in Chesham — and what a delightful aspect this would have opened up as you traversed the streets in the centre of the town. Unfortunately, the Urban District Council of the time and the local land owners did not have the foresight necessary to see what could be done with these many historical small dwellings.

REYNOLDS YARD

The Watercress Industry

In the first half of the Twentieth Century Chesham was widely famous for the quality of its watercress which was dispatched from the town by railway to London and many other parts of the South of England. Many of the original cress beds in the Bois Moor Road area resulted from gravel extraction which was needed to provide the embankment in the building of the railway across the Moor in 1888/9 but other cress beds were excavated in Church Street, Amersham Road, Latimer Road, Pednor Road and Higham Road. At Weir House Mill in Latimer Road, now occupied by Messrs. McMinns Hardware establishment, a large number of beds were excavated and a huge output of cress was supplied each week. A small part of these beds still exists as a trout farm and a small amount of watercress is still grown in Millfields and Bois Moor Road, but the industry today is but a shadow of its former self.

WATERCRESS BEDS AT WEIR HOUSE MILL

Public Houses and Beer Shops

At the turn of the last century, Chesham, with a population of 8,000 had 80 pubs and beer shops, one for every 100 inhabitants, men, women and children. The biggest majority of these of course supplied only beer, stout and porter. Wines and spirits were almost unheard of at the time. At this time many of the pubs were open from 6am to 11pm and many a working man went to the pub for a beer on his way to and from work. The wages from the factories in the town were invariably paid on Friday evening (in cash of course) and it was not unusual for many wives to be waiting at the gate of the factory as their men left in order to make sure that they could obtain their housekeeping money for the week ahead before their menfolk had the chance to spend it in one or other of the pubs or beer shops. There were several instances of two public houses being next door to each other. Indeed, in the Market Square there were six in the space of 50 yards. The Stag in the High Street was always known as the "Secret Drinkers'" pub. This building was entered by a passageway. To the right was the public bar and to the left was a small greengrocer's shop. The secret drinker would enter the passage saying that he was going to purchase some item or other of fruit or vegetables but the story is that many took the right turn instead of the left turn and ended up in the public bar. Of course, the majority of pubs at this time were extremely basic in their furnishings. Sawdust on a bare wooden floor was the usual covering and such seating as there was was in the form of wooden settles or long wooden forms. Little flair was known or attempted. The usual light was by gas — in some of the pubs nothing more than a naked gas flame. Few women would enter the pubs at this time.

Chesham and the Civil War

Chesham played its part in the Civil War of 1642. It raised a troop of yeomanry which fought for the parliamentarians and these men are reputed to have despoiled some parts of the Parish Church as they held fanatical ideas concerning ornaments and idolatry. On and around the West Door of St Mary's (the door is around 500 years old) just where so many Wedding Parties now stand for their photographs, can be plainly seen to this day a number of holes caused by shot, some 50 in number. Whether the firers were shooting at the church as a means of desecration or whether they were firing at opponents sheltering in the lee of the door is not known but the fact remains that this now peaceful spot must have been anything but peaceful at the time. Rumour has it that Cromwell attended service at the Quaker Meeting House in Quaker Lane — now Bellingdon Road. Warwick and Pym made their Headquarters at Chesham at one time and were expecting Prince Rupert with his horses and troops to invade the town. The following is a letter written by them:-

"To all worthy frindes (friends) the deputy lieutenant of the County of Buckingham.

Gentlemen
We perceive by your letter to Mr. Burgess that you are in expectation to be set upon by some of the horse commanded by Prince Rupert and that you mean to stand upon your guard. We shall take the speediest course to relieve you with all the horse and dragoons we have ready. We hope that my lieutenant General Essex will be at St. Albans this night, from whence we do not know but more powerful supplies may be employed in these parts so we rest your loving frindes Warwick and Jo Pym.

3rd November 1642 about 9 o'clock".

Fortunately, Prince Rupert was defeated at the battle of Aylesbury.

An order came from the House of Commons on 18th January 1643 that three Parish Overseers, Samuel Blackwell, Daniel Weedon and Gabriel Odingsells — should collect £850 as Chesham's contribution to the War and bring the sum to Guildhall. What a sum to collect in those days! This was to help pay for the War. The order was fortunately later rescinded.

King Charles I after his capture was kept prisoner at Latimer House and was entertained there when fleeing the country. Later when Charles II was being restored to the Monarchy Chesham took its place in the welcome. Later in 1745 when Prince Charles Edward was marching towards London from Scotland, Chesham, as did many towns on his projected route, barricaded the streets with "carts, wagons and beer barrels collected from all available

WEST DOOR OF ST MARY'S CHURCH

sources". Fortunately, he was defeated before he reached here.

What exciting times. Can you imagine what the atmosphere must have been like in the town then? But Chesham has sometimes been called 'Sleepy Hollow'.

Roger Crabbe Chesham's Hermit

It may not be well known that the Mad Hatter of Lewis Carroll's Alice in Wonderland may well have originated in a Chesham character. This was Roger Crabbe who was born in 1621 and served for seven years in the Parliamentary Army during the Civil Wars. His skull was unfortunately cloven during the fighting and for a breach of discipline he was sentenced to death by Oliver Cromwell. The sentence was not carried out and he was released. He came to Chesham and opened a shop in the High Street near to the George Hotel as a "Haberdasher of Hats". He was always rather hostile to potential customers, and what trade he did was rather doubtful as he was always apparently looked upon as "odd" by local folk who on one occasion had him cudgelled and placed in the stocks on Pillory Green, now the Broadway. He wrote two rather odd pamphlets entitled "The English Hermit (or the One of the Age)" and "The English Hermit's Speech". He had not long settled in Chesham before he had a strange notion that it was a sin against his body and soul to eat any sort of flesh, fish or living creature or to drink wine, ale or beer. He subsequently felt compelled to following the injunction given to the young man in the gospels and closed his business, gave his property to the poor and moved to a small cottage at Ickenham, Middlesex. There in a rood of garden he grew bran, herbs, roots, dock leaves, mallows and grass. On this he subsisted, drinking only water. His living expenses were said to have

been three farthings per week. In the book "The English Hermit" is a self portrait cut in wood with the lines "Roger Crabbe that feeds on herbs and roots is here, but I believe Diogenes had better cheer". He was said to have been reduced to almost a skeleton in 1655 but lived on till 1680 by which time he had moved to Bethnal Green where he died at the age of 59, a good age for those days, especially considering his deprivations. He was buried in Bethnal Green Church Yard on 14th September 1680 and a handsome tomb was erected to his memory. In the book "Worthies of Buckinghamshire" published in 1888 it states "His works show that he was simply insane". His name is now perpetuated in Crabbe Crescent.

Lady Whichcote's Funeral

Many of us have seen the very large monument to Lady Mary Whichcote in the south transept of St Mary's. It almost totally obscures the light from the south window and cannot be considered particularly beautiful. The following account from the parish register at the time is of interest.

"On October 3rd 1726 was solemnised the funeral of Lady Mary Whichcote late wife of Sir Francis Whichcote Bart. from her late house in Boswell Court City of London to the Parish Church of Chesham in Buckinghamshire. The proceedings began with porters in mourning cloaks, hatbands and gloves, 2 King's drummers in scarves, hatbands and gloves, their trumpets covered with crepe and banners of Sir Francis and his Lady's Arms. These gentlemen in scarves, hatbands and gloves carried six pennons of the above said Arms followed by two trumpets as before. The hearse was drawn by six fine bay horses covered with velvet and adorned with escutcheons, feathers, etcetera. Following that about 30 mourning coaches with six horses all attended by footmen in mourning."

On arrival in Chesham (the journey from London is said to have taken the best part of two days), the cortège reached the door of St Mary's whilst the tail of the procession was by Weedon's almshouses in Waterside. The expense of this magnificence ruined Sir Francis financially. He was forced to sell his magnificent mansion Bury Hill which stood in what is now Lowndes Park (somewhere near the site of the children's paddling pool). The House was sold to the Skottowe family who remained in occupation until the mansion was demolished in 1804. The lady is buried in a vault in the south aisle of the church in a coffin covered in velvet which was contrary to an act of Parliament which decreed that all burials at that time must be in wool to help the then depressed woollen trade. The family name is, of course, perpetuated in Whichcote Gardens.

LADY WHICHCOTE'S MEMORIAL

Margaret Butterfield's Sermons

Mrs Margaret Butterfield who died in the parish in 1674 must have been a lady with a rather fine opinion of herself. In her Will she left a sum of money which was to be invested by her executors, the interest of such investment to be available for payments to the vicar of St Mary's to preach sermons in her memory glorifying her good works. The sermons were to be preached on the Wednesday next after the 6th day of September, being the date of her birth and on the Wednesday next after 28th October, being the date of her death. The vicar was to receive 3s 4d (17p) for each sermon. History has it that these sermons were preached up until almost the year 1900 when they were quietly dropped, her good works having been glorified for well over 200 years. The capital sum of the charity is now invested in £100 of Government Stock and the resultant small amount of interest goes into the parish funds. The Vicar and Churchwardens recently attempted to wind up the Trust after over 300 years and have the Capital sum added to a more appropriate Parish Charity.

However, the decision of the Charity Commissioners was that "the Trust could be wound up, provided that the Capital be placed to a Charity with *a similar objective to the original.* So the matter remains . . . !

Troubles in the 16th Century

At the time of the General Visitation of the diocese of Lincoln ordered by Bishop Atwater in 1519 the churches in Bucks. were in an extremely poor state. Of 150 churches on which reports were made, only 22 were returned as satisfactory. Complaints were made of style, including church plans, chancels, towers, fonts, books and churchyards and recording reports of Rectory houses in ruins, of people talking and gossiping during Divine service and non-distribution of alms among the poor and of the non-fulfilment of duties by Rectors and Vicars. At Hawridge the Rector was non resident and left his parish to be served by a "most unfit person" who thought more of sports than of the duties of his office. He lived out of his parish in Chesham and within Holy Week said the whole offices of the day, including Compline early in the morning to suit his own convenience and so that parishioners were unable to attend. He was justly dismissed by the Bishop and the Rector was ordered to reside in the parish.

A proclamation was issued by Henry VII on 20th October 1521 requiring Mayors, Sheriffs and officers to assist the Bishop of Lincoln in dealing with the heretics existing within the diocese. Thomas Harding was among a number from Chesham who were dealt with. In spite, however, of the heresy and low moral life of the clergy, frequent pilgrimages were made to the shrines of saints and to other places of religious interest. The local centre of devotion was the monastery and religious house at Asheridge formed in 1283 as a College of Bonhommes and the object they worshipped was a phial containing a few drops of what was believed to be the precious blood.

During the second year of the reign of Edward VI all images and objects of worship were removed from churches. Many ornaments, censers, etc were found in Bucks. churches and when the inventories were made, Chesham was placed among the richest. There is a document in the Public Record Offices setting out a lengthy list of some 60 items which were removed from St Mary's by one Richard Marres but it is known that many men in a like position to Richard Marres made fortunes by the sale of these items.

Chaos in the 17th Century

During the reign of Queen Mary there took place vehement persecution of Protestants and under Queen Elizabeth's reign people were imprisoned and fined for harbouring Papists. Vestments and altars in the Churches were laid aside. Elkanah Gladman, vicar of Chesham from 1639-1660 was a lover of a simple form of service and he even refused to wear vestments. The Rector of Chenies did likewise and even administered Holy Communion to seated communicants. It is recorded that Church services became more formalised, both preacher and people displaying a "lax and unconscientious style". However, the common folk don't seem to have been as frivolous on matters of observance as was their king. James I wrote a "Book of Sports" which was supposed to be read from the pulpits in Churches. This book gave much offence to the good folk of the area and vicar Gladman refused to read it from the pulpit. For so refusing he was suspended from his parish. In 1656 Dr. John Andrews, vicar of Beaconsfield, wrote to Sir John

Lambe who had suspended Mr. Gladman "for so doing you are appointed and cursed to the body of Hell for suspending Mr. Gladman of Chesham." The suspension was thereupon lifted. Churches were in a corrupt and muddled state, some members hoping for a return to Catholicism and some members preferring the then existent Protestant service. The inevitable result was the depreciation of Church life. An illustration of which is a record of Amersham Church which states "Holy Communion had developed into a love feast" on one occasion 3 rundletts of wine each containing 10 gallons was ordered for a communion service. At least the parishioners must have left the church in a happy frame of mind.

Local Justice in Bygone Days

In an entry in the book of Court Leet of Chesham dated 1552 we read "William Chase, farmer of Hundridge and Sir Robert Dormer, owner thereof. There came in at that time a couple of springbucks (deer) within the lordship and manor within the lord's living and the said William Chase killed one and they vacated the hamlet of Hundridge. One Jeremiah Payne killed the other within the Hamlet of Bellingdon. It is to be observed that on the next court following a Jury was empanelled. William Chase had two brothers, John and Richard serving on the Jury. These two presented William to the Jury for killing one of the two bucks and fined him 10 shillings, Jeremiah Payne was likewise fined for the other killing." What honest and impartial brothers would fine their brother 10 shillings — there was no collusion in those days!

In the middle years of the 19th Century Chesham was guarded by just one constable. It had no lock-up of its own and prisoners were either taken to the small lock-up at Amersham (still standing underneath the Town Hall) or, more usually, to the County Jail at Aylesbury.

Bury Hill Mansion

The fine mansion which formerly stood in the present Lowndes Park known respectively as Bury Hill and the Rectorial Manor was built in Elizabethan times and was the second of the two great houses which graced the centre of Chesham, the other being the Bury. The house was occupied for many years by the Ashfield family who were patrons of the living of the parish church. It later passed into the hands of the Whichcote family and finally to the Skottowe family. All three family names are infinitely perpetuated in Chesham today. The grounds of the mansion extended to the entire area of the present Chesham Park and also to the area on which Chesham Park School stands and a further area of land off Chartridge lane. The ornamental lake now known as Skottowe's Pond was excavated in the early 1700's. It was fed from natural springs and to this day has an overflow outlet piped to the river Chess. Within the grounds stood what later became known as the Park Farm (opposite the present Avenue House in Park Road) and at the foot of the grounds on the site of the present St. Mary's Way stood a Gazebo. When St. Mary's Way was cut through the base of the park the Gazebo in a rather dilapidated state was removed by the Town Council to their yard. At the time of writing — 1992 — this has been re-erected opposite the White Horse, Amersham Road, in the Watergardens. The demise of the house occurred in 1804 and two stories of this are existent:-

1) that the Lowndes family wishing to extend their territory purchased the house and land

BURY HILL MANSION (DEMOLISHED 1804)

from the Skottowes and immediately demolished all traces of the house; and

2) that the Lowndes family and the Skottowe family challenged each other to a game of cards, the loser to demolish his house. The Skottowes lost with the inevitable result.

In front of the site of the house, roughly on the slope below the Girl Guide Hut was a large circular gravel path surrounding an ornamental garden. In a very dry summer the outline of this path can be clearly seen. The fine avenue of elms which led through the grounds of the mansion from Blucher Street to the Parish Church was demolished in 1950 at the time of the outbreak of Dutch Elm Disease. On felling, most of the trees were found to be sound. The land of the estate remained in the hands of the Lowndes family until 1935. The public were allowed access 364 days each year but on Good Friday gates were erected at the Blucher Street and Bury Lane entrances and the park was closed for the day to enable the Lowndes family to retain ownership. In 1935 to commemorate the Silver Jubilee of King George V the lower part of the grounds up to roughly in line with the children's swings was given to the then Chesham Urban District Council amidst much celebration. The upper part of the park was purchased by the council in the immediate post 1939-45 era.

GAZEBO FROM THE GROUNDS OF BURY HILL MANSION

Workhouse Gardens

The area of land on the corner of Germain Street and Wey Lane known as the Workhouse allotments must be, without doubt, the most critically appraised area of allotment land in the town. The land is part of the gardens of the former Chesham Workhouse — now numbers 35-37 and 74-76 Germain Street. The latter was built in the 1500's to house the poor and needy of the town. By the early 1700's it had become too small and was replaced by the larger building mentioned above. The gardens formerly embraced also the land on which numbers 41-49 Germain Street are built. The soil is a very light loam of varying depth from 1-2 feet overlaying a solid bed of gravel. It is of course part of the bed of the great river which flowed down the Pednor valley through Chesham and on through Latimer valley in pre historic times many thousands of years ago. The soil is very hungry, needing much food and in a dry season it needs large quantities of water to sustain growth. But if well fed and watered then the returns of produce from the area are extremely large. The only source of water on the land is an ancient cast-iron handpump well over 100 years old but which springs forth without much effort a plentiful supply of pure spring water. The land is low lying so the water table is always fairly near to the surface.

GARDENS OF THE FORMER CHESHAM WORKHOUSE

Chesham's Almshouses

There are twelve almshouses in the town comprising four Weedon almshouses in Waterside, four Standring flats adjacent and four Francis almshouses off White Hill (behind the White Hill Centre). The Weedon almshouses are by far the most ancient, having been erected in 1624 by Thomas Weedon, draper of London, who was the son of Richard Weedon farmer of Pednor. Thomas left the sum of £301 to erect alms houses. This was later increased to £350. They were for occupation by four good and godly women of the parish. These dwellings have in recent years been modernised and are now up to present day standards. The Standring flats nearby were erected in the 1960's from proceeds of the Will of the late Mr. W.J. Standring a member of the firm of Francis & How, solicitors. The Francis almshouses were erected by members of the same family in the Victorian era and are now held by the Cordwainers Company of the City of London.

WEEDON'S ALMSHOUSES

St Mary's Church Clock

The present clock in the tower of St Mary's was made in 1728 by one Thomas Vernon, member of the Worshipful Company of Clock Makers. It is a very simple form of birdcage clock in a cast iron frame. Two faces on the walls of the Church face respectively the High Street and Church Street. The reason for this being that when the original clock in the tower was erected in the 1500's the town comprised little more than these two streets. Watches and clocks in the home were a rarity at the time and anyone wishing to know the time, if he so wished, or was bothered, could always walk outside the home and, without moving very far, see one or other of the faces. It is known that a clock existed in the 1500's as in the record of the restoration of St Mary's in 1606 the sum of four pence was paid for

ST MARY'S CHURCH CLOCK

oil for the clock. The clock itself strikes only the hours. The chimes were added to commemorate the Golden Jubilee of Queen Victoria in 1887 and were made at the Steam Clock Works at Derby. The *Chesham Examiner* of the time stated that the cost of the chimes was £100 which was paid for the parishioners of the town who had "long desired that such chimes be erected in their church tower". The chimes comprise the quarter, half, three-quarter and hour chimes plus the playing of the hymn tune "Days and Moments Swiftly Flying" which is played at 12 noon and 12 midnight. This tune was chosen by William Walton, organist at the time of Hinton Chapel who suggested it was appropriate and also because the tune only needed six notes, that being the number of bells in the tower and each of the notes could be struck. The words of the hymn — a rather mournful one of the Victorian era — are worthy of repetition:-

Days and Moments quickly flying
Blend the Living with the Dead
Soon will you and I be lying
Each within our narrow bed
Soon our Souls to God who gave them
Will have sped their rapid flight
Able now by Grace to save them
O that while we can we might
Jesu Infinite Redeemer
Maker of this mighty frame
Teach O Teach us to remember
What we are and whence we came
Whence we came and whither wending
Soon we must through darkness go
To inherit Bliss unending
Or Eternity of Woe
Life passeth soon; Death draweth near
Keep Us Good Lord till Thou appear
With Thee to Live; with Thee to Die
With Thee to reign through Eternity.

The four spinelles of the clock and chimes are hand wound by St Mary's verger three times each week entailing the ascent of some 30 stairs. The clock is officially an eight day model but due to the wear and tear of the centuries if it is left for more than two days it begins to lose time rapidly. It is said to be the sixth oldest tower clock in England which is still in working order. There are others no longer in working order on the floors of cathedrals and abbeys and churches around the country. If any of the bells in the tower have for any purpose to be removed then the clock, which stands on the floor below the bells has to be bodily removed to permit access to the bells through the trap door below and above. This last occurred in 1980 when a new No 4 bell was installed. The removal of the clock, which weighs about half a ton, took less than one day but to reinstate it to its proper position and to reassemble the many weights and pulleys controlling the chimes and to get the chimes into good working order took two weeks.

The Animal Pound

At the junction of Amersham Road and Waterside in Red Lion Street stood the Chesham animal pound where, throughout the middle ages, when lands were rarely fenced or hedged, animals found straying were impounded pending their redemption by their owners. The actual pound, an oval fenced area stood in what is at present the centre of the road. An owner wishing to reclaim his animals had to pay the sum of 1p for a small animal or two pence for a large animal to the Lord of the Manor of Chesham Higham and Chesham Bury. On a wall near the site of the pound stands a plaque as follows:- *Here stood the pound of the Manors of Chesham Higham and Chesham Bury in which animals found straying within the manors were kept.*

PLAQUE COMMEMORATING THE POUND

The Flood of 1918

In May 1918 there occurred a tremendous thunderstorm centred on the hills above Pednor and Ballinger. The majority of the water flowed down the Pednor Valley carrying all before it some three or four feet deep. When it reached Pednor Mead End, the lower part of Church Street, the lower part of Germain Street and Moor Road, many houses were inundated. The inhabitants hastily removed as much of their belongings as they could to the upper storey but a large amount of damage was done to furniture and carpets. Indeed story has it that many carpets were afterwards taken down to the river edges to be soaked to remove the vast amount of mud with which they had been impregnated. I believe that to this day there are still water marks halfway up the wall of the downstairs of certain houses in Pednor Mead End and Church Street. The

AFTERMATH OF FLOOD IN CHURCH STREET (1918)

SNOWFALL OF 1926

torrent eventually found its way down through the Chess valley to Latimer and Chenies and very little damage, apart from the water, was done to property. By the following day the water had subsided but the trail of devastation took many months to be removed. Due to the fact that this happened during the 1914-18 war, little, if any publicity in the local papers could be given to the matter, it being deemed as of no national importance as such matters were in war time.

The Great Snowfall of 1926

In March 1926 occurred the heaviest snowfall in the district for many years. Snow fell heavily for about a week compounded by strong winds. Chesham was effectively cut off by road. Of course, at the time most roads outside the town had high hedges along their boundaries and the drifted snow settled between these hedges effectively blocking all transport. Chartridge Lane, the houses along which ended at the top of Park Road with few exceptions, was effectively closed for several weeks and had to be dug out by hand. Fullers Hill Road to Hyde Heath was similarly closed together with the roads to Amersham and Latimer. The train service was somehow maintained but bus services, which of course at the time were rather few, were halted for a considerable period. Fortunately, at that time the town was largely self supporting so there was no shortage of food and life was maintained at a reasonable level although people who normally travelled to work away from Chesham had enforced holidays.

Chesham in War Time

In the 1914-18 war many troops were stationed in and around the town. Many of these were billeted in private homes. Training took place in the Park, on the Moor, where a considerable length of railway was laid by the Royal Engineers, and also in Upper Pednor Road where a series of trenches were cut which remained in evidence for some 20 years. Certain evacuees came from London although there was no organised evacuation at this time but Chesham became temporary home to a considerable number of refugees from Belgium who fled their war ravaged country. Many families retained strong links with the town for years following the war and a substantial number of marriages took place between Chesham men and Belgian ladies who were resident in the town.

For probably the only time in its history, members of a European Royal Family resided temporarily in the Town, at Germains, in Fullers Hill, being Prince and Princess Andrew of Greece, parents of our present Prince Philip.

In the 1939-45 war things were on a much larger scale. From the day war broke out, 3rd September 1939, hundreds of children were brought by train from London and billeted in various homes throughout the town. The schools became somewhat overstretched and although overflow schools were established in various public, church and chapel halls, children's education had to be reduced to half a day — Chesham children in the mornings and evacuees in the afternoons, or vice versa. Some families took their children back home after a comparatively short period, certainly long before the London Blitz began but other children remained in the town throughout the war and as adults still return to see their host parents to this day. A large number of army camps surrounded the town at Pipers Wood, Ley Hill, Latimer, Great Missenden, Swan Bottom and Flaunden among others. The Bury in Church Street became a divisional Headquarters, the Lowndes family being literally turned out of the family home. A large camp was built in the Bury Grounds. Various canteens for the soldiers' use and entertainment were established, the principal one being in the then Equity Hall which was opposite Broadway Baptist Church in the Broadway. For probably the only time in its history a Jewish Synagogue was established for the town in the Cricket Pavilion in Amy Lane where several Rabbis ministered to their flock and a number of marriages took place. Later the Football ground too was occupied by an Army Field Hospital. In spite of its proximity to London, Chesham did not suffer badly from bombing. Bombs fell in Germain Street in 1940, in Pond Park in 1941, and a number fell in fields and woods surrounding the town. In the first two instances two persons were killed. Throughout the war years the town was grossly overcrowded. Indeed, on a Saturday night when the soldiers descended on the town centre for recreation and entertainment, hardly a square foot of space could be found. Later in the war years the US airforce established a base at Bovingdon from whence Flying Fortresses flew to bomb Germany and the US army took over the camp in Pipers Wood. As considerable numbers of US personnel also descended on the town a few fights and skirmishes took place among people of differing persuasions.

The blackout was rigidly enforced by the air-raid wardens throughout the war, blackout material being made freely available to householders and woe betide anyone showing a chink of light from a window, the warden would very soon be knocking on your door.

Chesham Hospitals

Until late in the Victorian era there was no such thing as a local cottage hospital. Most illnesses could be treated at home by the local doctor, if you recovered, so be it, if not — you died. Amputations were often carried out on the kitchen table with very rudimentary instruments. Anaesthetics were also rather primitive and history had it that many a patient was held down by neighbours and relatives whilst his arm or leg was sawn off. Of course, the large teaching hospitals existed in London. Before the coming of the railway in 1889 patients requiring such hospital treatment were conveyed by horse and cart. It is often said that if you withstood the rigours of the journey to hospital you usually recovered. The original Cottage Hospital was erected in the 1880's and catered for all types of operation and illness. The present hospital was erected after the 1914-18 war as a memorial and has continued to serve the town and district ever since. Prior to the coming of the NHS in 1948 the hospital had to be funded entirely by local efforts. Many townsfolk belonged to a "penny a week" scheme for which collectors would call regularly and various factories would collect from their employees. There were two major fund raising efforts during the year. Firstly, the Hospital Fete held in the grounds of the Bury on the last Thursday in July. During the afternoon a large variety of stalls were in operation together with rides for the children and various games and side shows. At dusk a very fine firework display was mounted at the farther end of the Bury Lake in the Grove which joins the main gardens. Hundreds of townsfolk started to assemble as dusk approached and at the firing of the first rockets those remaining at the fete would join the assembled throng. It was always said that the occasion was the originator of many of the town's romances. The second major fund raising effort was the carnival procession held in September on a Saturday evening when the town was virtually closed for the occasion. Chesham fire brigade recruited fellow brigades from far and wide and these formed the bulk of the procession together with many other floats and individual entries. Collecting boxes were rattled along the entire route and the resulting proceeds always amounted to hundreds of pounds. A further effort for the Hospital took place during the peak egg-laying season of March to April. Many local folk at this time kept a few chickens in their back yard or garden and in egg week a large marquee was set up in the centre of the Broadway to which people brought any surplus eggs they could spare. These were taken to the hospital and preserved in waterglass to be used for the benefit of patients throughout the year.

The earliest fever hospital, known as the pest house, was erected in the mid 1800's in Bellingdon Road (near the corner of Deansway) where persons suffering from contagious diseases such as typhoid, tuberculosis and other fevers were sent. The road alongside this pest house was for many years known as Pest House Lane (now, fortunately, re-named Bellingdon Road).

In the early years of the present century, a new corrugated iron Isolation Hospital (painted red) was erected along the Vale — just beyond Brown's Depot — and this remained in use until the late 1930's after which Aylesbury Isolation Hospital was used.

Some Gleanings from the Parish Registers

1727:
17 persons buried this year of the smallpox and also one Quaker carried to Amersham. In all 137 burials.

Jan 26th 1729:
Burials
William Geary brought from London and buried in the middle alley of the Church almost between the seats belonging to my Lord James Cavendish and that of his Grace the Duke of Bedford. (Who could William Geary have been to merit such an important space inside the Church?)

1729:
Buried this year 181 of which number 12 died of the smallpox and a great number of others with the pleuritic fevers. (The most fatal year discoverable in the registers to this time.)

24th July 1673:
Married — Thomas Carter of Amersham parish to Alice Hayes of Chesham having been ye widow of *four* husbands.

16th June 1654:
We allow to Mr Benjamin Carter ye seat on ye north aisle in ye chancel of Chesham abutting on ye seat where Michael Sear now sits with ye corner behind ye pillar adjoining to build a seat for himself and his wife at his own appropriate charges.

Signed by the Vicar and Churchwardens.

(Let us remember that at this time there were few seats in the Church on the floor but a bench ran round the wall for the aged and infirm — the majority of the congregation would have stood throughout the service — anything up to three hours.)

2nd Jan 1721:
Mr Matthew son of Mr John and Elizabeth Chase, owner of a house and tanyard situated and being near the upper end of this town of Chesham was buried on Monday ye 2nd day of January 1720 in a piece of ground called Great Meadlots about a mile to the west side of the field with his head westwards and near the hedge adjoining to the lane as ye go to Bellingdon by the order of his sad father and to the admiration of all people.

Finally, they treated them rough in the early 18th Century viz Jane Gray a vagrant beggar was taken begging in this town of Chesham and was whipped according as the law directs on February 12th 1703. Also Thomas Hund, a vagrant beggar was also whipped as the law directs on 28th July 1709.

The Development of the Town

The original settlement of Chesham is believed to have been in the area surrounding the present Market Square and for centuries right up until the industrial revolution during the Victorian era the town comprised little more than High Street, Church Street, Germain Street and Blucher Street. Waterside was of course a separate hamlet. The built up area finished at the foot of Hempstead Road (now White Hill) and beyond this were just a few isolated farms and cottages. The Sportsman pub (not the present building) was situated on its present site and nearby was a group of three houses in the centre of the already wide road opposite the site of the present Emmanuel Church. Beyond this, going towards Tring was Taylors Farm (off Cameron Road) and Vale Farm at the entrance to Vale Road. Industry began to arrive in the town in the 1850's and 60's and this was followed by a vast expansion of houses mainly to rent to house the workers in the various factories. Let us remember that at the time men liked to live very near their place of employment especially as factory hours were often 7am to 6pm with half a day on Saturday when they finished at 4pm. This resulted in the building of George Street, Alexander Street, Higham Road, Sunnyside Road, Gladstone Road and parts of Severalls Avenue, Townsend Road and much of Broad Street and Berkhampstead Road. All these were built by or around the turn of the century. The next expansion took place in the 1930's. This came as a result of slum clearance when many of the yards and alleys leading off Town Centre streets were ruthlessly destroyed and most of the inhabitants re-housed on the newly built Pond Park Estate. Although these were modern houses with bathrooms and toilets many of the people removed did not take kindly to their new surroundings. Also, during the 1920's houses for sale began to be built fairly widely. Examples of this are much of Chartridge Lane, Lowndes Avenue, part of Bellingdon Road and part of Hivings Hill. The next expansion or explosion came in the post-war era of the 1950's. During these years Chessmount, Hilltop and Broadlands Estates were built for sale and Great Hivings Estate was built comprising both local authority and private homes. Since the completion of most of these schemes in the 1960's there has been little further expansion of the town, there being a great shortage of building land due to the exigencies of the green belt. Present development comprises largely of in-filling on small sites or the demolition of one or more large properties to make room for a large number of smaller flats or houses.

Development of the Town's Industries

Until the outbreak of the 1939 war the town contained virtually only the traditional "Chesham" industries, i.e. those associated with timber and boots. There were some dozen or so boot factories large and small and the same number of woodenware factories turning out both brushes, brooms, traditional wooden spoons, seaside spades, bowls and domestic woodware such as egg cups, breadboards etc. There were also two toy factories, one producing wooden toys, the other producing mainly stuffed toys such as teddy bears. In 1940 with the bombing of much of London's industry various small companies arrived in the town and set up factories in any space available, even the town hall contained one. With the return of peace in 1945 many of these factories did not return to their origins but remained mainly on new sites in the town where they expanded rapidly and today we see a wide cross-section of industry probably as wide as any town of similar size in the south of England.

Sport in the Town

Until 150 years ago organised sport as we know it today was totally unknown. The earliest recognised club in the town was Chesham Cricket Club which was formed in 1848 and first played on a field in Higham Mead (off Higham Road) where they remained until they transferred to their present ground in Amy Lane in the 1880's. Football began to be played by teams from various churches and chapels. The present Chesham United was the amalgamation of Chesham Town FC formed in the 1880's and who played in Bellingdon Road and later in Berkhampstead Road and Chesham Generals FC formed at the General Baptist Chapel in Broadway and who played in Missenden Road. The two clubs amalgamated in 1919 and for the first 13 years of their existence shared the ground with Chesham Cricket Club. This resulted in a shortening of the seasons for both clubs and in 1931 the new ground, the present home of Chesham United began to be constructed. It was opened in September 1932 and since then the two clubs have peacefully existed side by side. In addition to the two major clubs there were both football and cricket leagues in the 1920's and 1930's comprising mainly teams from places of worship and various factories. Each league boasted some 20 or so teams and all were from within a radius of some 4 miles of the town centre, so little travelling was involved, let us remember that the usual method of travel to an away game for either cricket or football was by bicycles. For football you went in your football kit with ordinary clothes over the top, played on some decidedly muddy field and at the end of the game put your clothes on again and cycled home. For cricket it was usual to travel already changed in the usual whites carrying your boots on your cycle. On summer evenings at the completion of the match many cricketers would make their way to the town centre to swap notes on the afternoon's performance, let us remember that the shops were open until 8pm on a Saturday. The league cricket fields often left much to be desired. There were two in Missenden Road, one in Pednor Road, two in Chartridge Lane, one in the Vale Road, two in Lye Green Road together with other venues scattered around the perimeter of the town.

Public Entertainment

Until the late Victorian era virtually all entertainment centred on the home, songs round the piano, etcetera, or at the occasional concert in the town hall or one of the Church or Chapel halls. The first purpose built public entertainment building was the skating rink located in Red Lion Street (on the site of the present DSS office) in the early years of this century. This was a wooden building with a wooden floor on which roller skaters practised their skills. This only lasted until approximately 1920 but before its demise magic lantern shows were held there. These were the forerunners of the cinema. The first cinema, known as The Empire, was erected at the top of Station Road by 1909. This was soon superseded by the Palace (later the Astoria) which stood on the site of the present Superdrug Store in the Broadway. In 1936 the Embassy was erected in Germain Street and the two cinemas ran successfully side by side but under different

FAIR IN THE BROADWAY CIRCA 1920

SKATING RINK, RED LION STREET (LEFT OF PICTURE)

CHESHAM GENERALS' FOOTBALL GROUND 1914 BERKHAMSTED ROAD

ownership until the 1950's when the Astoria was closed. The Embassy continued on its way until the early 1980's when, due to drastically falling audiences, the building was closed and demolished. Another form of entertainment were the three annual fairs. These, for centuries, were held in the Broadway in April, July and September. They were charter fairs and dated back to the 13th Century. For many years they were purely cattle and hiring fairs, farmers would bring their beasts to be marketed at the fair and right up until the 1930's beasts were tethered in Blucher Street, Germain Street and Church Street on the occasion of each fair. The hiring fair was for domestic and farm servants to offer themselves for employment. For centuries a servant was bound to his or her master for one year only. At the completion of that year they could, of course, remain in employment if agreeable to both sides but, if they wished for a change, the servant would parade himself or herself at the hiring fair wearing a certain colour favour in the hat which would indicate that they were available for hire. A prospective employer, after looking them over and assessing their capability would offer employment in the coming year. If accepted the servant would be given a shilling to spend. Originally this could only be spent in one of the local hostelries of the town but in the 1800's various side shows began to appear at the fair, usually priced at 1/2d or 1d and at these the servants would spend their shilling. From these early rudimentary amusements grew the sophisticated rides and dodgems which we know today in present fairs. The fair (which by this time had become entirely for pleasure) remained in the Broadway until the outbreak of war in 1939 but traffic of course had increased by this time and the fair became something of an anachronism although space was still found for galloping horses, chairoplanes and dodgems together with lesser side shows in the centre of the Broadway. With the coming of the blackout in 1939 fairs were, of course, closed down and with the return of peace in 1945 the council offered the Showmen's Guild the use of the Moor for two or more days on the occasion of each visit. This was accepted and remains the pattern to this day.

Markets

For three or four hundred years Chesham had a weekly cattle market, usually held in the centre of the town where farmers brought their livestock to sell and to purchase anew. During the early 19th Century other wares began to be sold on a weekly basis, usually Tuesday, in and around the market hall which stood in the present day market square and was later enlarged to become the town hall. For many years until the outbreak of war in 1939 a number of stalls were set up on Fridays and Saturdays in the forecourt of the town hall but, unfortunately, the war put an end to this. The town hall, which was used during the years of the war as an ARP control centre, and as a factory fell into a sad state of disrepair in the 1950's. Unfortunately, although termed the town hall it never belonged to the town and was always in private ownership. By the late 1950's the building reached a dilapidated and dangerous state and was finally demolished in 1962 much to the regret of many townsfolk. It was felt that had the building been taken into public ownership it could have been restored to its original condition and become a prominent feature at the entry to the town from Amersham. The market clock which had crowned the town hall for around 100 years was demolished and taken into the care of Chesham Urban District Council. In 1974 on the change of local authorities this passed to Chesham Town Council. Now, some 18 years later the clock

MARKET IN TOWN HALL SQUARE 1920's

has been re-erected on a large column in the centre of the market square very near to its original site. The market now held on a Wednesday was re-established some 10 years ago in a small way. It is at present held in the Albany Place car park and has extended to Saturdays as well. The number of stalls remains rather small and, at the time of writing, does not show signs of increase.

Bus Services

The very first public bus service to operate in Chesham was the horse bus to and from Berkhampstead which was established very soon after the railway reached that town in 1838. In 1845 when the railway reached Rickmansworth another horse bus service was established. Both of these ran to meet each London train during the day, usually about four times and continued in operation until the railway eventually reached Chesham in 1889, over 50 years later than the neighbours. With the advent of the motorbus the Amersham and District Bus Company originated a service between Chesham and Amersham in the early 1920's. Services soon proliferated. The Amersham service was extended both to High Wycombe and later to Windsor. Other bus companies set up and ran services to Tring, Aylesbury, The Lee, Great Missenden, Hemel Hempstead, together with coach services to and from London. In the early 1930's competition became acute and it was obvious that none of the bus companies would survive. A fares war broke out and at one time the fare to Amersham was one penny single and two pence return. In 1934 London Transport was set up and assimilated all bus companies within 30 miles of the capital. This meant farewell to all the local companies excepting Rover providing a service to and from Hemel Hempstead which happily still survives today and the Lee Collins bus service which provided a service to Chartridge, Ballinger, Lee Common up until the 1950's. The coach service to London run by, at one time, three separate companies also

AN EARLY BUS IN RED LION STREET

engaged in a fares war and about 1935 the single fare to the West End of London was 1 shilling (5 pence), the return fare being 1 shilling and 11 pence. All these coach services were wound up at the outbreak of the 1939-45 war but London transport provided an hourly coach service from Chesham to London until about 10 years ago. Now we have the commuter coaches which provide a morning and evening service to the City and West End.

Holidays

Until the 1920's there were no real holidays as we know them today. The simple reason being that paid holidays had not been instituted. For the general run of the population such events as Sunday School, Church or Chapel and Club outings to local beauty spots were the only means of a change of scenery. Burnham Beeches was a favourite spot together, later, with Windsor. Until the advent of the motor charabanc in the early 1920's all such outings were by wagonnette. Of course, the few landed gentry took holidays to such resorts as Brighton and Torquay by train and a few, a very few, ventured as far as the continent, usually northern France. By 1930 holidays with pay had become the norm. Either one or two weeks at such favoured resorts as Southend, Brighton and Clacton. The latter in the years leading up to the 1939 was a great favourite with Chesham people, especially during the fortnight shut down of the majority of the factories which took place the last week of July and the first week in August. The journey to Clacton took about 2½ hours and, including fare on the underground across London, the return cost 12s (60 pence). On arrival at the resort (few people had booked) the search for accommodation began. Board residence was quite a rarity, most holiday makers opting for bed and breakfast or the taking up of an apartment which you rented for the one or two weeks, purchased your food locally and the landlady would cook it for you. A schoolboy with a truck would convey your luggage from the Station to a suitable establishment whilst you followed behind him on foot. This, of course, saved such things as taxi fares.

Wages at the time were somewhere in the region of £2 per week and people were not naturally big spenders whilst on holiday. Indeed, I know of one gentleman, alas no longer with us, who on his week's holiday to Clacton spent the princely sum of 6 pence, that being on a new collar from Woolworths. Nowadays, of course, destinations for holidays become ever wider — the other side of the world is now popular!

Chesham Parish Records

In 1537 Thomas Cromwell who held the office of Vicar General under the King decreed that all Parish Churches should commence to record the events of baptism, marriage and death. Prior to this date little, if anything had ever been written down. St Mary's records commence in July 1538. For the first 100 years they were written on loose sheets of parchment of varying sizes but in the early 1600's all these entries were transcribed into a register and the recording of events has continued right up until the present day. In early days when everyone was a member of the parish church the records presented a true and full picture of the parish but with the advent of non-conformity and the re-establishment of the Roman Catholic Church an increasing number of the parishioners worshipped at one or other of these places and so by the 1700's the parish records did not present a full picture of the population. In addition to the personal events the registers contain a surprising amount of information concerning events in the town. A few still come to light. Some statements of apology and a large number of records of collections made in the Church for other Churches in England and Wales which had fallen on hard times due to storm, tempest, outbreaks of contagious disease and fire. Some of the collections were as follows:-

8th June 1662
Gathered in the Parish Church of Chesham towards the repairs of the Parish Church of Bolingbrooke in the County of Lincoln the sum of Four shillings and Three pence.

15th June 1662
Gathered in the Parish Church of Chesham for Anne Royston the Relict of John Royston, Parson of Shaw and Donnington in the County of Berks, the sum of Four shillings and Eight pence.

29th June 1662
Gathered in the Parish Church of Chesham for the loss of John Melvich of Cresswell in the County of Staffords the sum of Five Shillings and Three pence.
(Three special collections in one month!)

5th March 1769
For Sheepy Magna Church, Leicester   1s 4d
12th March 1769
For Market Bosworth Church Leicester   1s 8d
29th March 1769
For Hedgerley Church, Bucks from House
to House   18s 0d.
(This one apparently merited special attention as Hedgerley was nearby).
(Again three special collections in one month.)

1769
For Honiton Fire, Devon   6s 0d
(Honiton Church was destroyed by fire, and a large

plaque in the Church commemorates this, and the help given by other Churches, to this day.)

In 1978 the Parochial Registers and Records Measures came into being. This Measure said that

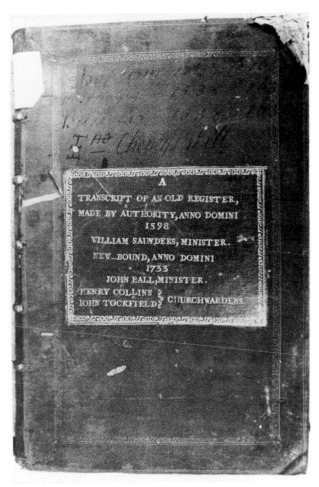

FIRST PARISH REGISTER (COVER)

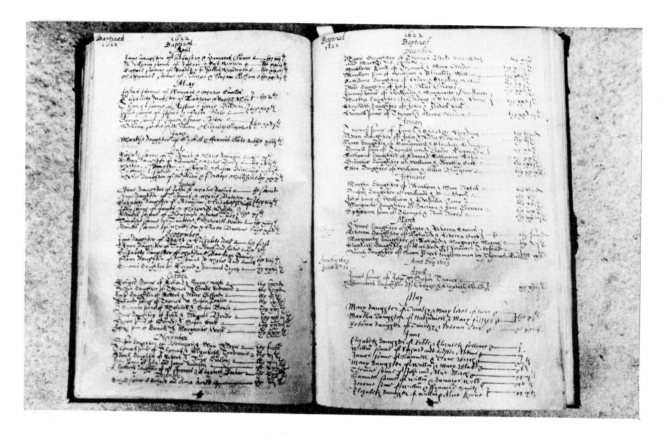

FIRST PARISH REGISTER

all Parish Records and Registers over 100 years old should be deposited in City or County record offices unless the Church concerned made application to retain them locally. It was felt at the time that St Mary's records were very much a part of Chesham's history and permission was granted by the Diocese (one of only a handful of parishes within the Oxford Diocese to obtain such permission) for their retention in St Mary's provided that a temperature and humidity controlled safe be purchased in which the records could be kept. With assistance from the Town Council such a safe was acquired and the Registers are stored in this safe to this day. They are much referred to by various persons researching their ancestry and are put on view to the townsfolk usually once a year when they evoke a large amount of interest.

Mills on the Chess

In the 1700's water mills began to be established on the river Chess as they were on most waterways in the country for the grinding of corn which had been grown on the local farms. Four water mills were built in rapid succession. Amen Mill, later known as Amy Mill which stood at the foot of the hill from Amersham, Lords Mill in Moor Road, now sadly only a wreck of its former self, Cannon Mill in Waterside now completely demolished and Bois Mill in Latimer Road now converted into a private house. In addition to this Weir House Mill in Latimer Road (now a hardware depot) was

AMY MILL

established as a paper mill. There are stories of another mill in Water Lane but the exact site of this is not known. All these mills depended for their power on the flow of water in the River Chess. Most of the mills ground corn until the 1950's, Lord's Mill being the last to work. It is a pity that at least one of these mills was not restored and kept as a reminder of an era not long past.

Early Days of Flying

In the 1920's it was a rarity for a 'plane to pass over Chesham and on hearing the noise (and believe me they were noisy) most people would run from their house to have a look. In the early 1930's two pioneer aviators, Alan Cobham and Henry Seagrave each established a form of Flying Circus which visited towns throughout the country in the manner that travelling fairs and circuses do today. Two sites were used on their visits to Chesham. One in Upper Pednor Road and the other now occupied by Hilltop Estate. Flying displays were given with intrepid aviators walking on the wing, looping the loop and performing various daring feats. Passenger trips for the sum of 10s. (or £1) were soon instituted in planes carrying a dozen or so passengers. For 10s you were treated to a trip of some 10 minutes duration which circled the town from end to end and was a great thrill for those taking part. Visits of these flying circuses ceased at the outbreak of war in 1939 when aviators had more serious matters on hand and, of course, when peace returned, flying became more and more popular until today it is the every day means of transport for anyone making a journey of any length.

Street Games

Today it is the exception rather than the rule to see children playing the traditional English games in the street. The general reason of course being there is far too much traffic and also parents have to be much more aware of the whereabouts of their children. Fifty years ago it was the done thing on summer evenings after school to play marbles, tops, hoops and fourwheelers for boys. Hopscotch for both boys and girls and skipping almost exclusively for girls. Hopscotch courts were chalked on many a pavement and boys with home made fourwheelers, a wooden box on an old pram chassis, would descend any hill or slope where momentum could be obtained. Marbles were originally of the clay variety but later the glass marble more or less took over and provided many varieties of colour on the street and in the gutters where most marble matches were played. Many boys also made or acquired a substantial truck, usually a Tate & Lyle sugar box on a pram chassis with a pushing handle affixed on the box. These trucks fulfilled several purposes for running errands, for fetching shopping for mother or other relatives and also for manure gathering. At the time many horses still patrolled the roads of the town and horse manure was regarded as a great fertiliser for local gardens long before artificial fertilisers. Boys would go round with their truck complete with broom and shovel and collect any droppings on the street before they got trodden into the ground by passing vehicles and a usual price for a truck full for your garden was about 3d or 4d.

Observance at Funerals

Up until half a century ago a funeral would bring forth far more observance than is the case today. Firstly, if anyone was known to be dying in their home it was the custom to strew the road outside with straw or sand to deaden the noise of the horses hooves as they passed by on their business. Following a death the blinds of the house concerned

EARLY FLYING AT CHESHAM

FLYING !!
AT BURY FARM, CHESHAM

Passenger Flights from 5/-. DAILY 10 a.m. TILL DUSK.

MONDAY, TUESDAY & WEDNESDAY
JUNE 30th, JULY 1st and 2nd.

SPECIAL ATTRACTIONS each evening at 8.

Thrilling Exhibitions of STUNT FLYING, including
Looping, Spinning, Rolling, etc., etc.
Also Thrilling and Daring Feats by an Acrobatic Aviator and
Stuntist who will

Walk Along the Wings in Mid Air

You have seen such Stunts on the films. Have you seen
them in reality? Do not miss it, you cannot see it elsewhere.

ADMISSION 6d. :: Children 3d.

WOLVERHAMPTON AVIATION CO., LTD.

were tightly drawn until after the funeral. Until the 1920's the use of a glass hearse with black horses was quite common. Messrs. Darvell of Waterside were the owners of such a hearse which was frequently in demand. Motorised hearses then became available and today are almost exclusively used. When a cortege left the home of the deceased on route to church or cemetery (cremation was virtually unknown) all the neighbouring houses would draw their blinds in sympathy and as the cortege passed along the streets pedestrians would stop, turn towards the road and men would remove their hats as a mark of last respect.

Floods in the Vale

In the 1920's and 1930's and indeed in a lesser way right up until the 1960's nearly every winter brought considerable flooding in Vale Road from the foot of Hawridge Hill southwards towards the town. The Vale which by its name acted as a natural funnel for the waters pouring off the various hillsides had no drainage. Therefore the water found its natural passage downhill towards the centre of the town where it eventually was swallowed up by the manholes and sewers. Several times during the 1930's the Vale became a complete river, the water covering every inch of road and by the end of each winter the tarmac surface had been almost totally destroyed. The floods even reached down Berkhamsted Road as far as the foot of Eskdale Avenue and on several occasions even reached to the Broadway. In the post war period with the erection of the pumping station at the foot of Hawridge Hill which was to provide a water supply for Aylesbury the surface water was taken up at its source and the floods gradually became a thing of the past although even today in a very wet spell Vale Road often becomes more water than road.

Former Industries in the Town

In addition to the traditional boot and brush factories Chesham has during the last century been the home of a very varied pattern of works. A Silk Mill formerly stood in Waterside between Hospital Hill and Gordon Road. This building later became the Royal Bucks Laundry which, together with another laundry in Eskdale Avenue provided the necessary services to the population before the advent of washing machines and Launderettes. A century ago a rope works stood in the vicinity of Queens Road. A basket making works stood on the corner of Townsend Road. A factory making men's braces formerly stood in the High Street near to the Post Office, later relocated to Bellingdon Road. A ladies' handbag factory was for many years until the 1970's located in Alma Road. Many ladies in Chesham to this day still possess a handbag manufactured there. Two toy factories were, for many years, present in the town, one at the foot of Amersham Hill and the other in Waterside and I am sure there are to this day many teddy bears still existing which were made in these factories. Two printing works formerly graced the town, one in the Broadway and the other recently demolished works of Page & Thomas in Germain Street. In the early part of this century there were of course several Wheelwrights and Coach makers providing equipment for the horse-drawn carriage trade. There were several shoeing forges to cater for the many horses which were in commercial use and for a time we even had a bicycle factory in Fosters Garage in the High Street which turned out the very sturdy Albatross bicycle, a very heavy machine, obviously built to last.

Street Traders

A century ago and indeed up until the 1950's street traders were very common. Door to door hawkers sold various items of sewing materials, simple jewellery and trinkets. The rag and bone man paid a weekly visit to every street in the town announcing his presence with a piercing cry. Most rags and bones were sold for a few coppers but certain enterprising merchants gave live goldfish to children in return for a substantial bundle of rags. The muffin man appeared on his rounds, usually on a Saturday afternoon, so that you could purchase some tasty muffins to toast for Saturday tea. Another often heard cry was that of the town crier who was employed by the local council to announce to the population that various public services were about to be disconnected for a short period in order that works could be carried out. He would also announce fairs and fetes, dinners and other such public occasions. I believe his normal fee for "Crying" an event was six pence.

Roads which have changed their Name

A number of roads in the town have, for various reasons, changed their name over the centuries. Bridge Street became Germain Street so named after Germains, the considerable mansion which stood in Fullers Hill. King Street was named after King William IV. The whole of this road and Amy Lane, its natural continuation were formerly Amen Lane. Bellingdon Road was formerly Quaker Lane from Blucher Street to the Quaker Meeting House and beyond there became Pest House Lane after the Pest House or Fever Hospital which stood at the corner of the present Deansway. Vale Road was for centuries known as The Bottom or Chesham Bottom and Eskdale Avenue, before being united at its centre in the early 20th century was Eskdale Road at one end and Mafeking Road at the other, so named after the battle of Mafeking in the Boer War of 1899-1901.

Some more Gleanings from the Parish Registers

PENANCE
John Catling, a Bookseller, performed Private Penance in this Church for Defamation, and Joseph Ware, Apothecary, performed Public Penance in this Church, both on 29th May 1757.

THE PUBLIC APOLOGY
In Volume 7 of the Parish Registers appears the following:-
I, Henry Body, Clerk of the Parish of Chesham, do acknowledge and confess that I have scandalously abused the Revd. John Ball, Minister, and Mr. Richard Twitchell, Churchwarden of the said Parish of Chesham, for which I do hereby declare I am heartily sorry and humbly ask their Pardon in this Public Manner, and do sincerely promise that I will never more defame them or either of them for the time to come, but will endeavour to behave myself with the utmost decency, good manners and civility towards them and all others by Lawful Governors and Superiors, as witness my hand this 14th day of February 1761.(Signed) Henry Body, Clerk of Chesham. Witnessed by Richard Cherrington Apothecary and John Hatton, Innkeeper. (One wonders what went on in the Parish before this Apology was made!! The fact appears that Mr. Body did not remain in office for long after this event — Matthew Archer was appointed Parish Clerk on 17th June 1763.)

Happy Days!

I have in my possession a Poster (printed by M. A. Garlick of the Printing Office, Chesham) giving Notice of the Annual Festival of the Chesham Parochial Schools to take place on Thursday 10th August 1854.

Proceedings commenced with a Dinner in the Park at 1pm for the Children, followed by a Tea for Visitors at 5pm, for which tickets could be obtained at a cost of 1/- from Mr Carden, Mr Sear, Mr T. Gomm or Mr Climpson. Throughout the afternoon, the Band of Her Majesty Queen Victoria's Second Life Guards would play, by kind permission of Col. Williams.

In the Evening, in the Parochial School Room, a Selection of Haydn's "Creation" would be performed. The principal Vocalists being Miss Clara Henderson, Mr G. Perren and Mr R. Farquarson from the London Sacred Harmonic Society, together with "An efficient Chorus" and the Life Guards Band. The Pianist was Mr W. Birch of Amersham and the Conductor Mr Surman, Founder of the Exeter Hall Oratorios.

Tickets were 1s 6d unreserved, 2s6d reserved and 3s for Central Reserved. Each ticket purchaser would be presented with a book containing the words of the Oratorio and 16 pages of the Music. Doors open at 7.30, music to commence at 8.00 and conclude at 10.00 with the National Anthem.

Hatchments in the Parish Church

St Mary's Church has ten Hatchments — few Parish Churches have more, many none at all.

The Hatchment originated in the Low Countries and is a debased form of the Medieval Achievement — being the Shield, Helm and other accoutrements carried at the funeral of a Nobleman or Knight. The Hatchments were locally made, and it was customary for one to hang outside the deceased's house during the period of mourning and afterwards placed in the Parish Church. The practice began early in the 17th Century but has now died out. St Mary's has one of only three 20th Century Hatchments known in Bucks., that for William Lowndes who died in 1905.

All were originally hung in the Nave of the Church but were removed in the Restoration of 1868/9. After this six were rehung in the South Transept followed later by the seventh to William Lowndes and the remaining three, being badly worn and torn, were put into store and remained there for over 120 years. In 1990 all ten were beautifully restored as a memorial to a parishioner, seven being replaced in the South Transept and three on the East Wall of the South Aisle. Of the ten they comprise seven of the Lowndes family, two of the Skottowe family and one of Newe Barwick.

The Skottowe Family

The Skottowe family, who lived at Bury Hill Mansion from 1726 to 1804, were always involved in Public Service.

The family is well documented in a book "The Heart and the Tree" by Philip Skottowe, which may be found in Chesham Library and the Memorials and Parish Registers confirm details of the family as follows:-

Coulson Skottowe Esquire
Joint proprietor with his father the Duke of Bedford of the Great Tythes of the Parish and late Colonel of the Militia of this Country.

If private virtue calls for our regard and domestic happiness be the lot of men, to him be the tribute paid.

He departed this life after lingering decay on the 21st of April 1784 respected and regretted by all his acquaintances and particularly to be lamented by the inhabitants of this Parish. He was buried in linen on the South Side of the Communion Table, close to the wall, age 65.

Mrs Ann Skottowe
Widow of the late Coulson Skottowe Esq., whom she

she survived only three months and two days. He died on April 21st, she July 16th 1784. She was possessed of many good qualities and the greatest of these was Charity, on account of which particularly she must be a loss to this Parish, as no object left the house unrelieved, and to women in labour, that stood in need of it, she gave childbed linen and money. She was buried in the same vault with her late husband, being placed upon his coffin. Aged 60 years.

Both entries are marked "Paid £5 for burial in Linen".

Thomas Skottowe Esquire

Brother to the late Coulson and John Skottowe Esquires. For many years he was Secretary to the Province of South Carolina in America, a situation said to be worth £2,400 per annum but which he was obliged to relinquish upon the breaking out of the unfortunate American War. The loss of that place and his Estates there in consequence, was made good to him by his and numberless other people's ruin in that business. (Lord North) by the ample salary of £200 for his own support and the bringing up of seven children. He died of the Gout in the Stomach, with which disorder he was almost without comparison afflicted. His remains were deposited in the vault built for his Brother John and family. Aged 52. Buried 1st November 1788.

Family descendants still occasionally visit Chesham — a group from Canada came in 1992 — and showed much interest in their history. What a pity that the family name has not been perpetuated in a Road in the town the only one among the occupants of the two Great Houses not to have been so remembered!

Former Roads

Many of the older residents will still refer to the road leading to Amersham — properly Amersham Road — as New Road; now it was once new, but that was in 1828, when the old road to Amersham named Beech Lane was closed. This ran from the foot of the Hill — just beyond Flint Cottage — behind Chesham Bois Manor, then through the Woods to appear at what is now Mayhall Lane by Bois Avenue. From there the road crossed Chesham Bois Common, descending through the present Hervines Park, to arrive in Old Amersham near the Football Ground. Much of the route can still be walked as a Public Footpath.

The present Trapps Lane which leaves Waterside by Christ Church was an old road to Boxmoor and Hemel Hempstead. It is a bridleway and footpath from Waterside to Botley, where it is now called Bottom Lane, thence across Ley Hill Common to Bovingdon and Boxmoor. Approximately 1½ miles along its length from Waterside stood the hamlet of Big Round Green, comprising a row of cottages. These were last occupied in the early years of this century, and only a small wood now marks the site. The cottages of course had no public services whatever.

The old road to Little Hundridge is still a bridleway and footpath leading off Upper Pednor Road about 1 mile out of the town and is now known as Blind Lane. This rises steeply up the hill, passes Barnwood Farm and emerges in Little Hundridge Lane.

These old roads still have a flint base, are now much overgrown and were never more than a cart's width. They were mainly used by packhorses.

Another First for Chesham

There lies buried in St Mary's Churchyard the body of one Daniel King, who died here in December 1768. Daniel was obviously one of the pioneers of the Sunday School movement in this country, as his tombstone shows him sitting on a chair, holding a large Bible, and in front of him sit three children.

Sunday Schools are always reputed to have been pioneered by Robert Raikes of Gloucester in the 1770's — 1780's but Daniel obviously pre-empted this by some years. Let us remember that, at the time, there was no "ordinary" education for children in this area — the first National School in Townfield Yard was not built until 1828 — and, until this School opened, the only education available was by paying at a "Dame" School. Very few parents could afford the fees for this, small though they were, and many children obtained the first rudiments of education in Sunday School, where Bible Reading and simple Arithmetic were taught.

Daniel's tombstone is located near the Chancel Door on the south side of St Mary's. It is of soft Sandstone — like most of the ancient Memorial stones — and after more than 200 years has become rather weathered, but the picture can still be clearly seen in a good light — especially on a sunny morning.

A Life of Service to Chesham — A Pleasant Memory and an Honoured Name

To many now in Chesham and its environs John Foot Churchill is but a name. To many others he is a pleasant and honoured memory. To those in the latter category who knew him well and held him in high regard while he lived and worked amongst us here, there are two names of that day and generation which stand out crystal clear — those of Dr. Churchill and Rev. Charles E. Boultbee, the Doctor and the Vicar. Each made their mark upon the Town; each was an outstanding figure; each had personality; and each had that independence of outlook and fearlessness of speaking which made actions and words carry full weight and which, if they had not been accompanied by a courtesy and quiet geniality would have made them uncomfortable folk to live with — as it was they were acceptable everywhere, honoured guests welcome in the house and home, men whom the people trusted and consulted. There are many who can remember the Doctor when he got actively about his wide rounds by other means than his tricycle (on horseback as an instance) but the mind recalls a sturdy figure pedalling steadily along the road, giving greeting, and being greeted, stopped here and there so that progress was not fast. His friend the Vicar loved his cycle and covered miles upon it, and the Doctor did also. Doctors were not so numerous then as now; the Doctor was in a peculiarly intimate capacity to his people; and Doctor Churchill was the friend and consultant of old and young, rich and poor. What a tremendous span of life he covered. He passed over one Thursday at the splendid age of 95 years. Most of his time spent in Chesham in activity and good works and he saw town and district undergo a wonderful metamorphosis. Dr. Churchill dated back to the time of Vicar Aylward and the great fever epidemic which played such havoc. As a young assistant to Dr. Faithorn he was in and out of the fever stricken houses and up and down the fever stricken town, and escaped fatal effects. The Doctor was reticent and never would recount "horrors" but when he was in reminiscent vein you caught a glimpse of that harrowing time; asked how he managed to escape so long he attributed with a twinkle in his eye to "Ann's hot soup". Ann was a fine servant of the Faithorn household and in those troublesome times her unfailing recipe for the young Medico was hot soup and it worked! In the neat and useful bit of historical data at the front of the Annual Report of Chesham Cottage Hospital 1927 it is stated: Mr J F Churchill retired from active service participation in the management of the hospital after being for 50 years one of its Honorary Medical Officers and subsequently Chairman of the Management Committee. That carries back to the 1870's and the Doctor was young in years when he first associated with the Hospital to which his Senior (Dr Faithorn) and later Miss Faithorn were so attached. That was a life's work for him, and to the last, while faculties lasted, his interest was of the keenest, and when, some fifteen years ago the Workers Hospital Committee was formed and the Contributory Scheme commenced to operate and when the scheme was in embryo Dr Churchill at an age when most men would seek release from added burdens went round the Town with Mr K Scott and did useful propaganda work. He associated himself with the Committee; he was a friendly Counsellor and genial worker; and always acceptable to the workers. To be made a Justice of the Peace was an honour to the Doctor and a recognition that he could and would serve his fellows where possible and he was active and regular in the discharge of his duties as a Magistrate but it really needed no such honour to add to the people's respect of him. One other little thing in regard to the Doctor's activities the mind recalls because of its significance of his outlook then is a useful work with which some are interested locally — The Soldiers and Sailors Scripture Readers. Dr Churchill was active in that because he had a great regard for the Service Man and for the young and certainly for the religious welfare. He has passed ripe in years and honoured in memory and of him it can truly be said that his work and influence abound. The purpose of this little sketch will have failed if it hasn't conveyed this — that Dr Churchill was a real friend of the Town and of the people. When he left the Town to spend the remainder of his time in the quiet of the Malvern Hills in the beauty and healthfulness he carried with him a host of good wishes, but social ties were not broken and while he was fit his old love the hospital was his keenest interest. The members of the Workers Hospital Committee never failed in their remembrance of him and regularly from their Meetings conveyed greetings to Miss Churchill to pass on to her Father.

(Dr. Churchill died on 24th March 1938)

(With acknowledgement to the Notes of the late Emma Harding)

Socialising at Bellingdon

On Thursday evening an 5th 1911 a very enjoyable and successful Social took place in the Bellingdon Mission Church. The Building was tastefully decorated by Ladies of the congregation and was crowded to its utmost capacity. Over a hundred were present, and much appreciated the programme prepared. The overture was played by Miss Elliot. Then came the Vicar the Rev. Charles E. Boultbee whose presence and well chosen kindly remarks were much appreciated. Songs by Mrs Williamson, Miss Elliot, the Misses Edith and Grace Walton, Mrs Goodwyn, Messrs. C and J Goodwyn, F Pearce and Dwight. Some humorous Readings were given by Mr A Gomm and Recitations by Miss Elliot and Miss Dulcie Sills. Pianoforte selections by Lilian Cook, Bank Farm and Miss May Sills, Bloomfield Farm, Miss Goodwyn, Bellingdon End Farm and Miss Grace Walton, Mount Nugent Farm acted as Accompanist. The piano was kindly lent by the Misses Brown (Pheasantries). A Phonograph was lent by Mr Newman and manipulated by Mr R James during the Interval, at which time Refreshments were handed round. The talent of Messrs. Goodwyn who received several encores was much appreciated and very greatly added to the pleasure of the evening. Mr J. F. Elliot presided and proposed a Vote of Thanks to all those taking part; this was seconded by Mr Ogborne husband of the School Mistress of Asheridge School, and Mr A. Gomm suitably responded. A profit of 12s 0d was realised; with this amount some new hymn and prayer books were purchased for use in the Services. And after that many more social evenings took place.

(With acknowledgement to the Notes of the late Emma Harding)